CLARENDON LIBRARY OF LOGIC AND
PHILOSOPHY
General Editor: L. Jonathan Cohen, The Queen's College,
Oxford

THE MATTER OF MINDS

THE MATTER OF MINDS

ZENO VENDLER

CLARENDON PRESS · OXFORD
1984

Oxford University Press, Walton Street, Oxford OX2 6DP

London New York Toronto
Delhi Bombay Calcutta Madras Karachi
Kuala Lumpur Singapore Hong Kong Tokyo
Nairobi Dar es Salaam Cape Town
Melbourne Auckland

and associated companies in
Beirut Berlin Ibadan Mexico City Nicosia

Oxford is a trade mark of Oxford University Press

Published in the United States
by Oxford University Press, New York

British Library Cataloguing in Publication Data
Vendler, Zeno
The matter of minds. —(Clarendon Library of
logic and philosophy)
1. Other minds (Theory of knowledge)
I. Title
121'.2   BD213
ISBN 0-19-824431-2

Library of Congress Cataloging in Publication Data
Vendler, Zeno.
The matter of minds.
(Clarendon library of logic and philosophy)
Bibliography: p.
Includes index.
1. Other minds (Theory of knowledge)   I. Title.
II. Series.
BD213.V46 1984   121'.2   84-15539
ISBN 0-19-824431-2

Typeset by Joshua Associates, Oxford
Printed in Great Britain
at the University Press, Oxford
by David Stanford
Printer to the University

Preface

I FIRST discussed the basic idea of this work in a paper entitled 'A Note to the Paralogisms' presented to the Oxford International Symposium in 1975 (later published in Ryle, 1977). Further details were added in a series of lectures given at the Sub-Faculty of Philosophy, Oxford University, during the Trinity Term of 1979. Previously, while a guest of the Research School of Social Sciences at the Australian National University in 1978, I composed the main part of what is now Chapter IV. Most of the remainder of the book has been written in Portugal in 1979, during which year I held a National Endowment for the Humanities Fellowship for Independent Research. I am deeply grateful to these organizations and institutions; any praise for the outcome should redound to them, while the blame should be mine alone.

My allusions to the environment, together with the examples given, reflect the changing historical and geographical background in which these pages were first composed. For sentimental reasons I have kept them untouched. I wish this inconstancy represented the greatest inconsistency in the work.

Most of what I say in this work concerns some functions of the imagination. And I leave to the imagination of the reader a few things that I should have said, but could not press into a modest book. I suspect, for instance, that the position I take here commits me to some sort of transcendental idealism. Also, that it has considerable implications for moral philosophy.

I have to appeal to the reader's patience too. He might get the impression, particularly in reading Chapter I, that I sometimes bite off more than I can chew. I wish to assure him that in the later chapters I duly chew the cud.

Although the idea of exploring the representation of other minds came to me independently, its development put me progressively into a Kantian frame of mind. So it is his influence that dominates the final product. Among the contemporaries, Thomas Nagel's work contributed the most to the views here expressed.

In addition, I acknowledge with gratitude the help, criticism, and encouragement of Professor R. M. Hare in the first place; he has shown interest in my approach from the very beginning. Another source of encouragement has been the late Professor John Mackie. I also have been helped by discussions with Professors Daniel C. Dennett and J. J. C. Smart, in spite of our remaining disagreements. And, of course, by my colleagues at this University, who were first exposed to my ideas as they developed, and through our discussions could not but influence them in many ways. In this connection I also have to mention two of my former students, Dr Patrick H. Murray and Mr William McKnight, who never tired of offering comments, help, and criticism. Finally I thank Ms Catherine Asmann and her colleagues, who carefully nursed the growing manuscript in the cradle of the computer.

Two of the six chapters of this work have been published in a somewhat different form before. Chapter III is an adaptation of the article 'Vicarious Experience', which appeared in *Revue de Métaphysique et de Morale* (No. 2, 1979), and Chapter IV of the article 'Reference and Introduction', which appeared in *Philosophia* (December 1981). In addition, Sections 16 and 17 of Chapter VI contain some arguments more fully presented in my paper 'Agency and Causation' forthcoming in *Midwest Studies in Philosophy*, vol. ix. My thanks are due for the gracious permission of the editors of these publications to use this material.

Z.V.

University of California, San Diego,
1983

Contents

Quand je considère la petite durée de ma vie, absorbée dans l'éternité précédente et suivante, le petit espace que je remplis, et même que je vois, abîmé dans l'infinie immensité des espaces que j'ignore et qui m'ignorent, je m'effraie et m'étonne de me voir ici plutôt que là, car il n'y a point de raison pourquoi ici plutôt que là, pourquoi à présent plutôt que lors. Qui m'y a mis? Par l'ordre et la conduite de qui ce lieu et ce temps a-t-il été destiné à moi? *Memoria hospitis unius diei praetereuntis.*

Pascal, *Pensées*, 88

I

Other Minds

1. MOST people would disagree with Descartes's claim that animals are mere automata. It just goes against the grain of common sense to think that, say, the pain of a cat, when someone steps on its tail, should merely consist of some nerve-agitation plus pain-behaviour. No, common sense insists, what this account leaves out is what matters most: the pain itself, and never mind the nerves and the behaviour. For, after all, this is why we are sorry for the cat, and other suffering creatures, in a way we are not sorry for a machine, no matter how complex or valuable (think of a fine car or a computer), when ill used or "tortured" by vandals or incompetents.

Yet we cannot show by scientific means that Descartes was wrong in this matter. For indeed science can find nothing but states of the organism: external or internal stimuli, conditions of the central nervous system, and behavioural reactions. Descartes's error, if it is one, is not a scientific mistake. The "pain itself" cannot be seen, and this is not because our microscopes are insufficiently powerful, either.

But then, since nothing else is left, is it not advisable to ignore our intuitions and assume that the pain, after all, is identical with the "pain syndrome" (stimuli, nervous-state, behaviour) or some part of it (the nervous state alone)?

People, as Wittgenstein noticed, learn the application of the term *pain* on the basis of certain observable conditions: the presence of external stimuli and behaviour. Yet sometimes these are missing, without rendering the attribution of pain false or meaningless. Think of slight headaches in us (no external stimulus, and often no behaviour), and of Spartans (no behaviour). Moreover, no avowals are necessary either: it is conceivable to suffer without complaint. Poor dumb beasts have to do it all the time. And, on the other hand, people at least are able to pretend to be in pain by displaying the usual manifestations at will. Thus the observable conditions involved in the learning of this term do not amount to real criteria, since their presence is neither a necessary nor a sufficient condition of being in pain.

This, as we know, is a fairly common situation. We learn how to use terms like *gold, acid, fish*, and so forth, on the basis of certain easily observable marks, which together amount to a "stereotype" of the natural kind in question. These marks, however, can be, and often are, overridden by the progress of science; they may turn out to be wrong, deficient, or superfluous. As a result of the scientists' work, moreover, the real essence of these things may be found, and expressed in terms of a chemical formula, atomic number, and the like.[1] Is it not conceivable, therefore, that with respect to pain, too, science will come up with the real criteria, the "essence" of pain, as it were, which has to be there if it is true that the subject is in pain? "Stimulation of C-fibres", or something like that?

Unfortunately, there seems to be a radical dysanalogy between "natural kinds" and pain or similar feelings. Consider such a term as *gold*. Once the scientific definition has been arrived at, one can ask the question, with respect to any chunk of chemically homogeneous matter, whether it is a piece of gold or not. That is to say, the scientific criterion applies universally. There are no exceptions; no cases in which one can sensibly assert: 'This is gold, no matter what the scientist is going to say'. Now, on the other hand, it is generally agreed that terms like *pain* are self-applied without criteria, and (except for marginal cases) without the possibility of doubt. If I have a splitting headache, I cannot be wondering whether I am really in pain or not; and I am certainly not going to ask the scientist to tell me, on the basis of his observation of my appropriate C-fibres, whether I am right or wrong. If there are no criteria, there are no criteria, scientific or otherwise.

But what about other people's pain or similar affliction? The same thing holds, for their sincere avowals take precedence over any other manifestations, and these avowals, once more, are made without evidence. Even if you honestly claim that your nugget is gold, the scientists may be able to demonstrate, to your own satisfaction, that it is but pyrite. It may look gold, but it is not. But if your tooth hurts, the dentist may point out that it is your jaw and not your tooth that is at fault, but no dentist, and no physiologist, can hope to convince you that you are not in pain at all: they will not be able to demonstrate, for instance, that what feels like pain is not really a pain but a tickle. What looks like gold may not be gold, what looks red may not be red, but what feels like pain is pain. And this is the real difference between

[1] See Putnam's 'The Meaning of "Meaning" '.

"objective" notions like *fish, gold, red*, or *hot*, and "subjective" notions like *pain, tickle, fear*, and the like.

Or again, to give a closer comparison, consider the concept of *being drunk*. This, too, is an objective notion, in spite of the fact that some subjective feelings are associated with it. In this case the subject's own judgment about his condition is by no means decisive. True, in most cases the subject can conclude, on the basis of various signs, that he is drunk, but errors can occur either way. Accordingly, it makes sense to say things like 'I must be drunk, though I don't feel it', or even to ask 'Do you think I am drunk?' Now with pain, such statements or questions are out of place. Thus, although the learning of both terms, *being in pain*, and *being drunk*, must begin in a similar way, i.e. through the recognition of certain syndromes consisting of stimuli and behaviour, for the full mastery of these concepts a further step is needed: the realization that the former, but not the latter, is self-applicable without evidence, that is to say, that the former is a subjective notion, but the latter is an objective one. And for this reason, as the police know so well, the condition of being drunk can be established by means of public criteria, and the delinquent's own protestations do not carry any special weight. Drunkenness is constituted by a certain physiological condition of the organism; pain is not.

Thus, the most the scientist can hope to establish is a fairly reliable correlation between the occurrence of certain nervous states and the experience of pain. His results are bound to remain on the same level as the prescientific marks: external stimuli (needle stuck in the skin) and pain behaviour (wincing, etc.). Their presence makes a prima-facie case for the attribution of pain, but does not constitute it. Now, the "excitation of C-fibres" is perhaps a more reliable warranty, but it cannot amount to the essence of pain either. For it, too, is an objective condition, publicly observable to all, whereas pain itself is but an appearance to a subject. The brain and the stimulated nerves *are* in the body, but the pain is only *felt* in the body by a subject. My toe, with nerves and all, is in my shoe, but the pain in my toe is not in my shoe.

'But if pain is a mere appearance,' someone might argue 'then the stimulation of C-fibres, or some such thing, can still be regarded as its essence, since in other things, too, true nature and appearance are distinct. Water is H_2O, yet it does not look H_2O for sure.' Notice, however, I reply, that the appearance of water you are talking about is a public appearance: what water looks, feels, and tastes like are objective facts, which can be listed in textbooks. All these facts, more-over, can be explained in a systematic and coherent manner on the basis of that chemical constitution: what water looks, feels, tastes like is a function of its index of refraction, specific weight and heat, freezing and boiling points, crystalline shape, and so forth; and all these data are derivable from the fact that water is H_2O. In other words, science can demonstrate that H_2O ought to look like that. But there is no way of deriving the phenomenal quality of pain, what pain feels like, from any physical, chemical, or neurological facts. There is no way of show-ing why certain conditions of the organism should be perceived as pain and others as tickle. Water looks different from tar, because . . .—and there comes an explanation in terms of physics and chemistry; pain feels different from tickle, because . . .—and the explanation is want-ing. The stimulation of C-fibres *happens* to be felt as pain; there is no demonstrable correlation between them.[2]

2. The situation is similar with colours. The different frequencies of red and blue light explain their different photochemical and other effects; yet they do not give any information as to what the colours red and blue look like. That the sky and the sea often look blue are also objective facts, explainable in scientific terms; what blue looks like is not. Accordingly, the perfectly colour-blind person who knows enough physics may be able to find out, by means of scientific tests, what things are blue, and may be able to predict what things will look blue in what circumstances; yet he will not be able to tell what looks blue to him, as we do, without tests, without criteria. And a perfectly insensitive person, if there is one, will not know, even with an exhaustive know-ledge of physiology, what pain is like, and, consequently, will never be able to say truthfully that he is in pain. Thus, the notion of pain is not like the notion of blue, not even like that of looking blue, but rather like the entirely subjective idea of looking blue to someone on a parti-cular occasion, "seeing blue" as it were, on the analogy of "seeing stars" when hit on the head.

The difference, therefore, between terms like *blue* and terms like

---

[2] 'Suppose we imagine God creating the world . . . To make the C-fiber stimula-tion correspond to pain, or be felt as pain, God must do something in addition to the mere creation of the C-fiber stimulation; He must let the creatures feel the C-fiber stimulation as *pain*, and not as a tickle, or as warmth, or as nothing, as apparently would also have been within His powers. If these things in fact are within His powers, the relation between the pain God creates and the stimulation of C-fibers cannot be identity.' Kripke, *Naming and Necessity*, pp. 153–4.

pain is the following. With *blue* it is the objective element that "wears the trousers", and the subjective element is a derivative one. There are things in the physical world that are blue, there are things that merely look blue in certain circumstances, and there are subjective experiences associated with the perception of things that look blue. A blue after-image, for instance, looks blue to the subject, because it strikes him in the same way as the colour of the clear sky, and other things that look blue.

Now, with pain the priority is reversed. The subjective condition (being in pain) wears the pants, and the objective marks, be they behaviour or states of the nervous system, are merely associated with it. As blue after-images are not really blue, but merely appear blue to the subject, so pain behaviour, or the stimulation of C-fibres, are not really pain: they merely suggest pain to the beholder.

One may speculate about the reason for this difference in priorities. The most likely explanation is the following. Most things in the world display colour, whether animate or inanimate, but only a small fraction of them are subject to sensations. It is more convenient, therefore, to give a name to the objective condition in the case of colours, and let the subjective element remain derivative. With pain and the like, however, since their most familiar subjects are beings capable of speech and thus avowals, the subjective aspect is endowed with a name, and the objective side is left derivative. Things, logically, could be different: *blue* might name a sensation, and things that normally cause it could be called *blue-producing*, or something like that; and *pain* could be a name for pain producing stimuli, pain behaviour (or, if you are really scientific, for the agitation of those notorious fibres), and what we now call pain could be called *pain-feeling* or something similar. As a matter of fact our language works differently; but this is not so important. What is important is the distinction between the subjective and the objective sides regardless of the naming game.

And one more thing: the realization that not only objective things have reality. Pain is mere appearance, but it is different from a tickle, and "seeing blue" is different from "seeing red". The colour-blind person misses something that we have, and Descartes's automata would not be real animals.

3. Let us return to the tortured cat and the tortured car, at least in imagination.

Take the car first. We can imagine, quite vividly, the scene . . . or recall one from memory. There is the car, shuddering and bucking, howling and whining, as the driver revs her up, grinds the gears, slips the clutch, and so forth. If you know a good deal about cars, your imagination can follow it up, representing the innards of the machine, the cylinders, the valves, the gears, and the rest, together with the punishment they receive, and the damage they may undergo. You may also connect the shudders, the squeaks, the roars, and the explosions, to the workings of the various parts. If you have a lively imagination you can fill in the details, but essentially the picture is complete.

Now the cat. The man's foot is on her tail, and she does not like it a bit. She snarls and whines, tries to scratch and bite, the fur is raised, and the ears lie flat behind. Again, the power of the imagination, at least in a physiologist, might fill in the picture by representing the interior of the cat: the muscles and the organs, the brain and the nervous system, agitated as they are, accounting for the furious activity displayed by the beast. Is, then, the picture really complete? Not at all, for Descartes was wrong, beasts are no mere machines: the cat, unlike the car, is in pain, and the man torturing her does not merely offend our aesthetic sensibilities as the car-torturer might do, but also provokes our moral condemnation.

'Just imagine what it must be like having one's tail stepped on.' And, in spite of the relevant differences in anatomy, I can. I have had my toe trodden on; it must be like that. And the fear, and the whole syndrome of wanting to stop it, to retaliate, to get away . . .

Right up to this last move, whatever I imagined about the car and the cat could also have been perceived by the senses. There are circumstances in which one sees cars and cats being tortured, and there are even ways of observing the inner workings of cars and cats under stress, in the machine shop or the laboratory. Thus, what I imagined could also have been observed, seen or heard, in an appropriate setting. The last move, however, is entirely left to the imagination. Even in the presence of a tortured cat or man, our senses will not perceive what they feel—the pain, the agony, the anger, and the fear—as they do perceive the shudders and the shrieks, and, by means of suitable instruments, the convulsion of the muscles, and the firing of neurones. What they feel, the pain and the like, cannot be perceived by anybody else; the very nature of pain is such that its total reality is exhausted in being felt by a subject. It is not *in* a subject as the nerves are, also available for inspection by others; it is *to* a subject, or *for* a subject, without a remainder, without an aspect open to alien perception; a mere appearance, in other words.

Nevertheless, we can imagine, or at least try to imagine, the cat's pain. Now, this exercise cannot consist in imagining seeing or hearing the pain, as there is nothing in it to be seen or heard; not even feeling it, in the way one feels the surface of a table, since, although a pain is something to be felt, it can be felt only by the subject who is in pain, without presenting a surface, as it were, to be felt by another. What one has to imagine, therefore, is being in pain, but this is surely not enough. When I sit in the dentist's waiting room and try to steel my nerve by imagining the pain to come, it is *my* forthcoming pain that I conjure up. What I am now called upon to do, or try to do, however, is to imagine the cat's pain: what it must be like, not for me but for the cat, to be in that situation. But, as we said again and again, pain is an entirely subjective thing, it has reality only to a subject. Thus I have to imagine being that subject to be able to imagine that pain: what it must feel like being on the floor, with a small furry body, and a tail stepped upon by a huge and hefty creature. By imagining being that animal one approaches its pain and other sensations and sentiments subjectively, the only way they can be approached.

To sum up, in representing the abuse of that car the flow of the imagination runs along a single track: roughly speaking, it has to show what the car and its parts look like *to an outsider* during that process. The abuse of the cat, on the other hand, requires a double track: what the cat and its parts *look* like, again from the outside, and in addition, what it must *be* like, *for the cat herself*, to undergo the process. And whereas the first track is but a substitute for sense experience, since whatever we imagine that way could also be perceived, the second track is proper to the imagination: what it represents is not something the senses too could perceive.[3]

4. Some philosophers will object at this point, if not sooner, that the theory of identity between mental events and physical states which I contended with thus far is too narrowly conceived, and, accordingly, the opposition I just sketched between "what can be seen" and "what can only be imagined" about another sentient creature is overdrawn. They will argue that what is essential about mental states—pain and other sensations not excluded—is not a particular physiological

[3] In using the notion of "what is must be like . . . " I am of course indebted to Nagel's works mentioned in the Bibliography.

realization in certain types of organisms (e.g. the excitation of C-fibres for pain), but rather an abstract functional state which accounts for the behaviour of the organism in a given set of circumstances. Thus whether the "organism" in question is composed of cells or transistors, its "beliefs", for instance, will amount to a physical condition incorporating in its own way a certain abstract state of a Turing machine. And similarly, some venture to add, even pain and other feelings can be attributed to all kinds of contraptions, provided their overt behaviour under appropriate simulation betokens a functional state identical with, or analogous to, our state of pain and other sensations. Now, since abstract entities cannot be seen, our inability to detect the pain of that cat, by means of microscopes and the like, does not show that it is a mere appearance, i.e. an entirely subjective thing. To use a crude analogy: the program of a computer, and the information it possesses, are not something to be seen in the way the wires and the transistors are; this does not mean, however, that the former things are only appearances to a subject.

I do not wish to contest the merits of functionalism as a theory of cognitive psychology. With respect to beliefs, intentions, and other "program-receptive" states, it paves the way to the "modelling" of minds, and thereby to a better scientific understanding of what advanced organisms are and how they function.[4] It has been pointed out, however, that such "intentional" states do not have a phenomenology of their own:[5] having a belief or having an intention, unlike being hungry or in pain, are not perceived by the subject as characteristic experiences of certain intensity—something that can be endured or enjoyed. And for this reason, whereas it is easy to imagine being in pain or being tickled, there is no way of imagining directly what it must be like thinking that the earth is flat, or intending to take Philosophy 14 next term. It may be possible, therefore, to account for these states in purely functional, and thus objective, terms, for there is no specific phenomenological residue left over. But with "program-resistant" features —sensations, feelings, and sentiments—such an account cannot work, simply because in these cases it is exactly the phenomenological content that is attributed to the subject in the first place: 'he is in pain' means that he has a certain specific experience, whatever else may be true about his nerves, or the functional state he embodies. And this

---

[4] The distinction between program-receptive and program-resistant features is found in Gunderson's *Mentality and Machines*.

[5] e.g. by Dennett in *Brainstorms*, p. 32.

experience is resistant to any objective representation. 'What it is like to be in that state' cannot be reduced to 'what that state is like', no matter on what level of abstraction the latter is described.

5. I just claimed that the exercise of the imagination is indispensable for the representation of a person or animal as a subject of sensation, feeling, and emotion, and not merely as an object of perception.

This claim may be challenged along the following lines. As one can see, or otherwise perceive, that an animal is healthy or sick, young or old, and the like, one can also see that it is angry, scared, or is in pain. If, for example, the circumstances and behaviour of that cat are as I described them, then it makes perfect sense to say that one can see that the poor beast is in pain. Accordingly, since what one can see one can also imagine, it is possible to imagine the cat being in pain without embarking on the second track, the subjective exercise, mentioned above.

My reply to this argument begins with an *ad hominem* move. Although the Cartesian theory of the automatism of brutes is at variance with common sense, it is, presumably, a bona fide philosophical position, not one that can be refuted by an appeal to common experience. No Cartesian would deny anything, for instance, that can be observed about the behaviour of animals. Therefore, since whatever we can see the Cartesian too can see, it is either not true that we can see that the animal is in pain, or, if we can, then what we see must be compatible with the hypothesis that animals are mere automata. Consequently the common sense view, according to which animals are no mere automata, attributes more than what the senses can reveal.

Descartes, of course, was clever enough to provide a distinction between the various senses of the term *sensation*, applicable to *pain* too.[6] What can be seen by observing the organism is sensation$_1$, which merely consists of certain motions of parts and particles. Over and above this, however, there is for us, but not for the brutes according to him, sensation$_2$, which consists of the first awareness, or consciousness, of pain and other sensations.

With this distinction in mind, I reply as follows. If you take *pain* as an objective notion (sensation$_1$), then indeed you can see that an animal is in pain. As a matter of fact pain is not an objective notion, however, and by treating it as such you leave out its real nature, which is entirely subjective. But if you really mean pain by *pain*, i.e. the subjective

[6] *Reply to Objections VI*: At VII, 436-7; HR II, 251.

experience (sensation$_2$), then you can see that an animal is in pain only in another sense of *seeing that*, which plays a role in such contexts as 'I then saw that the Germans are going to lose the war', or 'I see that he has no sense of humour'. Needless to say that this kind of *seeing that* has nothing to do with sense perception; it denotes an inference on the basis of certain evidence. For this reason it cannot readily be extended to sensory imagination. Try to imagine seeing that he has no sense of humour. If one means by *pain* what we normally mean by *pain*, then the sentence 'X sees that the cat is in pain' means that X has concluded that the cat is in pain on the basis of the cat's behaviour, and other observable features. And the Cartesian, who sees what we see, simply refuses to draw the inference. His position, right or wrong, is perfectly intelligible. Hence, for all we see, the cat may not be in pain, it may be a mere machine.

6. We disagree with him, of course, for we *know* that animals, and *a fortiori* other people, can suffer or enjoy life in much the same way as we do. Is the use of *know* here but a whistle in the dark? Do we really know? And all the failed arguments purporting to solve the "other minds" problem loom in the dark like so many tombstones: here lies the Analogy Argument, there the family of the Arguments from Language, and so forth. RIP. True or false, the Cartesian position, at least with respect to beasts, is intelligible. Can we say the same thing of the view of common sense?

Since the experiences we are talking about are entirely subjective, that is to say, their whole existence indeed consists of being perceived by a subject, the first question that arises is this: is it conceivable that there be other subjects besides me? How can one show such a possibility? Certainly not on the basis of what the senses reveal to us: what they can deliver are objective data alone; the testimony of the senses is bound to remain forever silent about subjects.

But where the senses fail, imagination might succeed. Not in the way of representing possible states of affairs in the world that also could be perceived by the senses, but, as we mentioned above, along the "second track", the subjective path. We can imagine what is must be like for the cat to be in such distress. And, in general, we can imagine being someone else: that blind beggar, that child, Helen Keller, or Napoleon. We might not be able to bring it off to our own satisfaction, but we can try without the threat of absurdity from the outset. Hence we see that being a subject, being an "I", is not necessarily tied to having the experiences I actually have. Subjectivity is not bound to the content of my consciousness: I can remove and replace as much as I want to, as much as necessary to represent the "mind" of that alien being, without the slightest harm to the self, to the "I", to subjectivity. There are other ways of being conscious too. Other minds are possible, therefore, since we are capable of intersubjective transference in imagination.

Thus, when we say that an animal is in pain, we can fully mean what we say, because we have an idea of what it must be like for another subject to be in pain. And when we deny the Cartesians' claims that animals are mere automata, our disagreement is not merely over words: we attribute something to the beasts that the Cartesians refuse to do, and we know, and so did Descartes himself, what that thing is. Without the possibility of intersubjective transference, however, we would have no idea what it would be like for someone else to have feelings and sensations over and above the organic and behavioural manifestations. We would not understand avowals of pain and the like, since we understand them now on the basis of our own condition, our own pain, and the possibilty of self-ascribing the term *being in pain* without evidence. And since we are able to transfer this whole condition to other human beings, we can understand what they say.

In that mindless world, however, the term *being in pain*, if it could exist at all, would indeed remain a purely objective notion denoting an observable syndrome, something like *drunkenness* or *smallpox*. But, of course, one cannot even speculate about language, as we understand it now, in a world like that.

It is the imagination, and the imagination alone, that saves us from solipsism, and makes it possible for us to attribute subjective states to other beings in the world, and for that matter, given the impossibility of a private language, to ourselves. In Kant's words: 'I cannot have any representation whatsoever of a thinking being through any outer experience, but only through self-consciousness. Objects of this kind are, therefore, nothing more than the transference of this consciousness of mine to other things, which in this way alone can be represented as thinking beings.'[7]

7. But this result, surely, is only the first half of the story. The question is not merely whether other minds are conceivable, but whether there are any. Granted, I can imagine what it must be like for the cat . . . , if that cat is a conscious being and no mere automaton. This *if* is a big

[7] *Critique of Pure Reason*, A347, B405, KS332.

if; maybe it is like nothing for the cat . . . My imagination, as in other things, may represent something which is not so in reality.

Notice, however, that in those other things there is a reality, accessible to the senses, at least in theory, which may be different from the way I imagined it. But in this case the only access to the "consciousness" of the cat available to me, or anybody else, in practice or in theory, is via imaginative transference. There is no "correction" possible from experience, or any other source. The role of experience is confined to providing the boundary conditions for the imagination: by revealing the physical condition of the cat, it limits my imagination as to what the cat must feel, *if* it feels anything. The same thing holds about people's avowals: without prejudicing the issue whether they are conscious or not, their words are nothing more than further elements of the syndrome on the basis of which I attribute pain or similar affliction to a subject, the very existence of which remains in doubt.[8]

Can I be wrong in attributing pain to a cat which shows all the signs of being in pain? Yes, possibly, if its cortex has been tampered with . . . This is irrelevant, however, since this fact again belongs to the objective order imposing one more limit on my imagination. Let us have then a perfectly normal cat, its tail being stepped upon, showing all the manifestations I described. Can I still be wrong? Yes, if it is an automaton, and does not feel anything.

Can I ever find out whether it is an automaton or not? No, since whatever I can find out about the cat belongs to the objective realm, whereas its pain and consciousness, if any, do not. This can be put in another way, too. In order to know that, say, the cat is in pain, the condition of its being in pain must be causally connected to my representation of its being in pain. Now since the very condition of being in pain is a subjective condition, it cannot stand in a causal relation to anything beyond the consciousness of the subject. Indeed, the scientific explanation of the cat's behaviour will never mention the feeling of pain as a factor over and above the agitation of nerves and the like. Therefore, in the ordinary sense of *know*, no one can ever know that an animal or human is in pain, or is not an automaton. Consciousness is not something to be *found* in another; it can only be ascribed to it.[9]

'Perhaps knowing is too strong—belief, with good reasons, might

[8] 'The verbal expression of pain replaces crying and does not describe it.' Wittgenstein, *Philosophical Investigations*, I, 244.

[9] Here I assume a causal theory of knowledge, which by this time is a respectable assumption. Anyway, as the next paragraph shows, nothing important depends on this point.

do . . . ' It will not, I reply, and for the same reason. No connection between pain and what we call the manifestations of pain can ever be established without the question-begging step of assuming that some animals showing these signs are conscious and are in pain.

'But then,' you object, 'how is it that those manifestations are called manifestations of pain? And, mind you, it is on the strength of that correlation, between pain and its outward signs, that we are able to learn the term *pain*, to be applied to others on the basis of evidence and to ourselves without it. Thus the very possibility of *pain* and other "P-predicates" in the language is based on the assumption that people and animals are not machines but beings endowed with inner life.'[10]

This argument fails, I reply, as all arguments pretending to prove matters of fact on the basis of language are bound to fail. I agree that the use of P-predicates in the language presupposes *belief* in the existence of other minds. For that matter, so does the existence of language *simpliciter*. But this dependence does not show that that belief is correct. The sociologist addressing the cigar-store Indian assumes that it has a mind, and the pious talk to God thinking that he exists. But one cannot prove the existence of God, or immortality, on the basis of religious language and the Book of Common Prayer. We learn our language, indeed, with the tacit and unquestioned assumption that there are other minds. And, given the possibility of transference, we understand what we assume, for we can represent to ourselves what other minds would be like. Yet, for all that, it does not follow that *de facto* there are any. After all, to play a Wittgensteinian game, we can imagine a tribe of robots, exactly like us in all outward manifestations, including "language" containing P-predicates, who, by hypothesis, would not be capable of feeling anything. This picture is in fact the scientific picture of mankind and its behaviour—except, of course, the last denial, the content of which is usually glanced over with a disdainful shrug.

8. 'But wait! Would that picture include you?' Why certainly, there is *that* robot, sitting at a desk and writing these lines . . . 'No, that cannot be you, since you at least are no robot but a conscious being.' Let us complete the picture, then, by adding my inner life, along the second track, in imagination: what it must be like being that creature sitting there with that body, and experiencing the world from his

[10] About P-predicates, see Strawson's *Individuals*, chapter III.

point of view. But, of course, I can do the same thing with respect to any other robot in the picture within the "boundary conditions", mentioned above, imposed upon the imagination by its physical set-up: think of robots eating, working, or watching TV; then think of handicapped automata, blind and deaf ones, and so forth; then of animal-like robots, such as that cat, and the rest. In this respect there is absolutely no difference between that robot sitting at that desk, and the others going about their business. There is no difference in the grounds of attributing consciousness: in each case I do it on the basis of physiological make-up, physical circumstances, and behaviour. And what I attribute is essentially the same too: in each case I imagine what it must be like for that thing to be in those circumstances and to behave in the way it does.

'But listen: you are *that* robot and not the others!' Yes, indeed I am. But what difference does it make *in the picture I imagined*? The fact that I am that thing and not another does not belong to the picture. Except for the richness of detail here or there, the same global picture would emerge even if I were Jimmy Carter or the Dalai Lama. Notice, moreover, that such a representation may contain everything that science and common sense attributes to the world; the robots are not robots any more, but people and animals.

The world is such that it contains beings which offer, as it were, anchors to subjectivity: Z.V. is one of them, Carter is another, and in a different way, and to a lesser extent perhaps, so is that cat. Each of these things offers a perspective, a point of view, from which the world can be perceived and experienced, enjoyed or endured. By looking at things in this way, one creates a representation of the universe containing certain beings endowed with minds, because, for one thing, that particular creature sitting at that desk has a mind, yet the picture does not attribute to him one whit more than to the rest, and for no better reasons: he is one of the many, and, as far as the mere idea of a mind goes, he is by no means "more equal" than the others.

'That *he* is *you*, however,' you insist, 'you not only imagine but feel your pains, and experience your other sensations and perceptions.' But so do the others, I reply. For, in representing those other minds, I do not imagine their experiences to be somehow fainter, or less real than mine; those minds do not appear more "bloodless" than this. Of course, I happen to have *this* mind and not another, *these* experiences and not others. But indexicality, the *this* and the *that*, does not add to or substract from the nature of anything. Indeed, *for me* it makes all the difference in the world that I am this man, and not someone else; but it makes no difference in the world.

If I imagine a world in which there are no cats, I imagine a different world; if I imagine walking on the beach now, I fancy a slightly different world; but if I imagine being Jimmy Carter, it is the same world I imagine, bodies, minds, and all, from a different perspective. And perspectives do not change the nature of things either. I am *at* a certain point of the space-time universe; but this realization does not add one stroke to the representation of the whole.

9. To use a fashionable idiom, in imagining being somebody else I do not have to create a different possible world; all that is needed is to view, through the power of my fancy, this very same world, nothing changed, from a different perspective. Yet, no doubt, in doing so, I imagine something which is not the case; yet what is not the case does not show up in the world I represent: not in its objective features to be sure, but not even in the minds I project for the organisms that license such a move. My mind is singled out in that image purely indexically, by mere "haecceity".

This reminds us, of course, of Lewis's theory of possible worlds, and his indexical view of actuality: the actuality of the world we inhabit is not an added feature which distinguishes it from other conceivable and imaginable worlds.[11] Existence is not a predicate, and actuality is not a property, of one world among the many. Each world is actual to its own denizens, and it is up to them to determine what exists in theirs.

I do not think that Lewis's conception of possible worlds can be squared with intuition, or can stand up to philosophical scrutiny. My main reason for objecting to it is based on a Kantian point: it is impossible to represent a manifold not connected to our world of experience by links of space, time and causality.[12]

This difficulty, however, does not apply to the representation of other minds in *this* world. The anchors of transference are bodies to be found in this manifold, and the alien perspective I assume in imagining what they must be experiencing is in fact dependent upon the objective representation of our common world spread out in space and time.

Nothing prevents us, therefore, from applying the indexical theory of actuality to the problem of other minds. Each consciousness is a

---

[11] e.g. in *Counterfactuals*, pp. 85–6.
[12] See my 'On the Possibility of Possible Worlds'.

"world" of its own, as such unconnected to any other consciousness: a "windowless" monad, something like a Lewisian possible world. Now, to each of us our own mind is the one which appears as the given, and from which we may depart on the wings of fancy to represent the others. In doing so, however, we are not merely guided by logical possibility, as Leibniz and Lewis proceed in setting up their possible worlds, but by the empirically and historically given existence of other organisms, and their conditions, warranting transference. We do not have to cope, therefore, with an infinity of possible worlds, the identity-conditions of which remain forever undetermined; nor are we faced with the problem of "counterparts" and cross-world identification. We are dealing with a finite number of organisms, and the inner lives we ascribe to them on the basis of empirical data.

10. But do we *have* to take this path at all? Cannot we leave well alone and remain satisfied with the physical world, as described by science, and bereft of minds altogether? Yes, we can, of course; there is nothing wrong with such a representation: there is no inconsistency, and no gap in the picture.

But what about *me*? I, for sure, am conscious, and my representation of the universe must account for that fact at least, even if I be alone in the world . . . All right, then, let us accord experiences to *this* body, as we said before . . . Which body? Mine, of course. But what makes a body my body? What does it mean to say that I am this man, Z.V., rather than Carter or the Ayatollah Khomeini? The answer is simple. Whom do I have to pinch to feel the pain? Myself, naturally, i.e. Z.V. Carter will not do. In general: this is the body whose projected experiences match my actual ones. I can imagine what it must be like sitting at that desk, holding a red pencil and staring at the wall, or casting a glance over the sea, where the tankers go by. And what I thus project I find in experience: the feel of the pencil, the sight of the sea, and so forth. In fact, I find more; features I could not project in imagination on the basis of the known condition of my body: the slight headache I have, the tickle in my nose, and the like. Thus I have a "privileged access" to my mind, which I do not have to the mind of Khomeini. But even these features appear integrated into the experiences projectible as pertaining to this body: the headache may be alleviated by *my* taking aspirin, and the itch by scratching *my* nose. They have to appear, furthermore, in time, that is to say, located in a sequence of inner events, some of which at least must correspond to the perceived state of my body. Short of such a connection, an experience would not count as my experience at all. Whatever I am aware of at any given moment is perceived as a feature of *my* mind, i.e. of the unitary consciousness attributable to this body.

What does it mean to say that I actually have, and do not merely project, these experiences? Simply this. When I project some experience —for myself or others—the sensory intuition, evoked by the power of fancy moving along the second path, *follows* the work of the understanding, and of the imagination operating along the first path. For example, in trying to represent what it must be like, subjectively, for Carter to be sitting in the Oval Office, I must first represent the objective situation in my imagination (along the first path), based upon my knowledge of the pertinent facts about him and that place. Only then can I proceed to imagine, along the second path, what his experiences must be like. In other words, the objective representation determines the subjective one. Now, with actual experience the order is reversed. The subjective experiences are given first to be integrated into a state of mind, which has to be brought into correspondence with the state of mind projectible for this body. Since, however, the given experiences surpass in many details the imaginary expectations based on the known conditions of this body and its environs, some progressive adjustment in the representation of these conditions may be necessary to keep the two aligned. Thus, whereas with respect to other beings the "fit" between the physical and the mental is one-directional, in my own case it has to follow a two-way street. If I see you being pinched, I imagine what it must be like—but if I feel a pinch I look for its cause . . . Actual, therefore, means given and not just evoked. And its being given is the cash-value of its "haecceity". As *this* world is said to be the one given in experience and not merely projected, so *this* mind is the one which is experienced and not merely evoked.

Still, if I am to find *myself* as a person in the world, i.e. a mind reflecting the conditions of *this* body, I can do so only through the application of a principle which directs me to assign experiences to all "deserving" organisms. For the recognition of this body as mine is the *result* of the application of this principle which is perfectly general in its scope. There is no way of singling out this body in advance for preferential treatment; nor is it possible to restrict the applicability of that principle to one privileged organism—since before its application there is no reason to favour one above the rest. I can represent myself as a person, therefore, only as one of the many organisms endowed with inner life.

For there has to be more than one such "deserving" body. As we mentioned above, the very possibility of endowing some beings with experience in one's imagination depends upon the recognition of certain bodily conditions warranting the attribution of such experiences. Now, in order to learn what these conditions are, one has to be exposed to a variety of bodies displaying these manifestations. To put it in another way: one would not have the concept of, say, being in pain, without having encountered organisms displaying pain-behaviour. If I were the only advanced organism in the world, my concepts, if any, of pain, of experience, of subjects, and of myself, would be quite different from what it is now. This much, at least, is clear from Wittgenstein's arguments against private language. Or, if we assume innate ideas of great specificity, then that lonely "me" would be on the look-out for company . . .

11. A last-ditch attempt to escape the force of my argument may be made along the following lines. 'Let it be granted that, in order to find yourself in the world, you must project experiences for all suitable organisms, so that in one of these projections you may recognize your current mental state. Then you will know that the method of projection you used, i.e. imagining what it must be like to be each of these organisms in turn is indeed valid for a single case, namely yours. For your experiences do conform to that projection. But then you still may doubt the validity of that method for all the other cases, since, as you admitted, you cannot have direct evidence: you can imagine, but not experience, their mental condition.'

My answer begins with a parable. In order to test the map-reading skills of a future officer, his instructor takes him in a closed van to a spot in the mountains, where he is released, provided with a large-scale map of the region, and asked to locate himself on the map. We all know what he has to do: imagine the perspectives corresponding to the diverse locations on the map, and compare them with the one he actually observes. His training and skill enables him to succeed: he finds the spot at which his actual perspective matches the one he evokes in fancy. Then he argues as follows, 'Now that I have discovered that I am here, I know that the map is correct for this particular location, that is to say, as far as I can see. But it still may be all wrong concerning features, if any, beyond my horizon.'

Now I ask: where does he point in saying 'I am here'? If at the landscape, then what he says is false. He did not *discover* that he is there;

that he knew from the outset. If at a spot on the map, then he is talking nonsense. Being "there" on the map presupposes that the *whole* map represents a region, which means that there are regularities connecting features and signs throughout. Granted, there may be errors here and there, but no map on which one can locate oneself can be wrong all over the place. To say, therefore, 'I am here on this map, which, however may be all wrong elsewhere' is absurd. The cartographic sceptic *cannot* find himself on a map.

The application of the story? In the first place, the task of finding oneself in the world cannot be fulfilled by saying 'I am the subject of these experiences' (thinking of one's current mental state). This observation has nothing to do with the world or one's location in it. The point is to be able to say 'I am this' (having in mind a specific part of the physical universe, namely an individual human body). But to be able to say that, one has to connect a unified set of experiences (a "perspective") with the physical conditions of a body. Now the only way of doing this is to project experiences ("what it must be like . . . ") for all bodies which license this move ("deserving" organisms), in order to find the one whose projected experiences match the experiences one actually enjoys. But once this is achieved, one cannot go back, as it were, and cast doubt on the validity of the whole procedure by saying things like 'The method works in this case, but may not in others', for doing so would amount to discarding the very "rule" by virtue of which one has found oneself in the first place. No *this* case ('I am this body') can emerge without a prior application of the universal rule. To mix Wittgensteinian metaphors, casting doubt on the general validity of the rule is not merely throwing away the ladder, but cutting off the branch on which one sits. Solipsists, other-minded sceptics, *could not* find themselves in the world.

My parable, of course, is just a parable. For one thing, maps can be checked for accuracy throughout, since they, as much as the landscape they represent, are observable entities. Minds are not; so no similar check is possible. The force of the parable lies elsewhere, namely in the realization that the map-reader cannot consistently deny the reliability of his map and yet locate himself on it. What he can do, however, is to decline the task altogether. In a similar way, the solipsist may consistently refuse to attribute minds to organisms, but only if he gives up on the *justification* of his own identity.

As I am going to explain in Chapter II, I do not claim that the principle of finding oneself in the world given in this proof represents the actual psychological process leading people to the recognition of who they are. What I offer here is a philosophical justification of such claims aimed at the sceptic. To him I say: I have shown that no self-containing world-representation is possible without the recognition of other minds, i.e. that the attribution of experience to all deserving organisms is a transcendental condition of locating one's body in the world, and thus recognizing oneself as a person.

12. Let us sum up, then, the main steps in our argument.

(a) It is possible to conceive of the physical world, including animal and human organisms, all without an inner life.

(b) We cannot show the existence of other minds on the basis of experience, since the data of experience are one and all objective.

(c) Within the limits of the "boundary conditions" given by their physical state, we can imagine for some advanced organisms what it would be like being those organisms.

(d) My body is the one whose projected experiences conform to my actual ones.

(e) This realization does not add anything to the representation of that body and that mind; they are singled out purely indexically.

(f) The recognition of this body as mine is the result of the application of a universal principle ascribing consciousness to all deserving organisms.

(g) Accordingly I can represent myself only as one conscious being among other conscious beings in the world.

Have I just proved the existence of other minds? Yes and No. No, because it is possible to view the world "purely scientifically" as it were, restricting one's concern to the realm of objective facts. In this case, however, I cannot find myself, as myself. Yes, on the other hand, for the following reason. Given this argument one cannot keep wondering whether or not there are *other* conscious beings in the world. You can find yourself in the world only as one conscious being among the many, the one to whose mind you have a privileged access. Since, moreover, the "other minds" problem, as the name shows, is motivated by this concern, the answer is more of a Yes than of a No.

'You cannot get away with this,' my opponent objects indignantly 'for your proof is something like an ontological argument deducing existence from a representation. You may represent other beings as conscious—it does not follow that they are. Suppose I have a hundred dollars in my pocket (or a beetle in my box). Then I imagine myself and you each having a hundred dollars in our pockets. It does not follow that you too have that money in reality. You see the analogy?'

Certainly I do, I reply. But I draw your attention to two crucial differences. If I do not have the hundred dollars in my pocket, this is an objective fact, which can be found out by suitable investigation. But what I imagine in performing transference is in perfect accord with all the facts and all the data. I do not argue, moreover, that those bodies are conscious because I choose to represent them as such, but rather that I *have* to represent them as such in order to be able to locate myself in the world. The fact that my argument is not an empirical proof (no such proofs of other minds are possible) does not show that it has to be an ontological argument. It is a transcendental argument spelling out an a priori condition of all self-locating world representations.

13. The world of science, the manifold of experience, is spread out before me like a gigantic map.[13] It does not contain yet any indication of where I, a conscious being, might fit into it. In order to find my place I have to light up certain points with the inner glow of subjectivity. In one of these illuminated "cities" I recognize myself through the privileged access I enjoy with respect to that mind: I inhabit that city, that conscious life is mine. This discovery, however, does not enhance the light of that spot, nor does it diminish or douse the glow of the others. I may wish, of course, to "peer" into those other minds, i.e. to extend the range of my privileged access. But then I realize that this is impossible: the unity of apperception means exclusiveness; perspectives do not mix. Minds offer no windows to look in from the outside. But I can imagine being someone else. In doing so, however, the same exclusiveness applies: if I imagine being you looking at me now, then it is to your mind that I fancy having a privileged access, and it is my mind which will be projected on the basis of my observed situation. One's total representation of the world, which contains conscious

[13] The representation of the world I am considering here is the work of the imagination. Yet it does not consist in one image, but in our ability to evoke sensory (mainly visual) aspects at will. As the memory of my house is not exhausted in one remembered glimpse, but consists in the possession of a "schema" which enables me to project some total or partial presentations of that house in imagination, so our ability to represent various aspects of the world is due to a "schema", which functions like a rule or prescription for the work of our fancy. Much in the same way as a computer, given the data defining, say, a regular solid, is able to project its appearance, in whole or in part, from a desired perspective on its screen. I shall say more about this topic in Chapter III.

beings, has to resolve into an alternation of being uniquely attached to the world at various points.

I conclude with a few reflections on the upshot of this chapter. We have demonstrated, in the first place, that the only way of conceiving the possibility of other minds is by means of imaginative transference. There is, furthermore, no way of showing the existence of other minds from the data of experience. In our total conception of the world, however, one cannot represent oneself as oneself without ascribing consciousness to oneself and to some other beings, without discrimination. There are, then, two crucial abilities upon which the whole enterprise depends: the ability to imagine being someone else, and the ability to imagine oneself in a detached way, as a being among other beings in the world. To put it paradoxically: one has to be able to represent another as oneself, and oneself as another.

II

Transference

1. IS IT indeed possible to imagine being somebody else? In the previous chapter we assumed that it is. Yet, in view of the crucial importance of this move, it is advisable to cast a closer look.

We may approach the subject by first visiting a half-way house: by considering a less radical exercise of subjective imagination. We often say things like 'If I were in Jimmy Carter's shoes I would . . . ', or, 'If I had been in Hitler's situation in 1940, I would have . . . ' Such speculations do not require full-blown transference: thinking about what I would do in Carter's situation does not require imagining being Carter. The point of such a reflection is exactly to draw a contrast between Carter's actions and what I would have done or would do in his place. Accordingly, I may continue my remark ' . . . but, of course, that would not square with his Southern Baptist conscience'.

The fact that people are sometimes sloppy in their speech and say things like 'If I were you, I would start reducing' does not make a difference, since even in this case the speaker may add 'but you like pastry too much'. And it would not do to reply: 'But in that case it would be *you* who like pastry too much.'

Nevertheless, in all these cases, if the speaker really means what he says, he has to assume in his imagination some of the elements of the person's situation in whose place he puts himself. In speculating, for instance, about what he would do in Carter's situation, he has to imagine being endowed with Presidential powers, living in the White House with all of its paraphernalia, having to deal with Cabinet and Congress, meeting the Press, keeping the voters in mind, and so forth. Some other items of Carter's attributes and circumstances are likely to be irrelevant to the purpose: his smile, Amy, his brother, and the peanut-farm, may be left alone, unless the point of the speaker's reflections are actions concerning them.

There seems to be nothing impossible about the task involved: the force of the imagination is powerful enough to put me, albeit vicariously, in any circumstances I can conceive. I can imagine, now, walking on the sea-shore, on the Acropolis, or on the moon; eating oysters, or being hungry; kissing Raquel Welch, or talking to Richard Nixon. Then why not sitting in the Oval Office, talking to Ham Jordan, signing bills, or giving a fireside chat? If I know enough, and my imagination is lively enough, I can elaborate on the picture to my heart's content; like a historical novelist or film-maker I can complete the *mise-en-scène*, and then ask myself, against such a realistic backdrop, what would I do in such a situation.

.Yet I have to take care, lest the very flight of the imagination which carried me thus far should frustrate the whole enterprise, by sweeping me past the point beyond which no contrast can be drawn between me and the person whose circumstances I assume. Because then, of course, there is no sense in asking what *I* would do in *his* situation.

Is there such a possibility? Yes, there is. Fortunately, however, what lurks as a danger to our present task will prove to be a blessing for another and more important one.

As I mentioned above, in thinking about what I would do in Carter's situation, it is not necessary to assume all of his circumstances in imagination. And, so long as I stick to that task, it is necessary not to assume some of his attributes. I must not appropriate, in particular, his personality and character; his opinions, prejudices, and hangups; his past experiences preserved in memory; and so forth. For what I am speculating about is what *I* would do in *his* situation with *my* character, conscience, general beliefs, and the like, precisely because these are the factors influencing conduct and choice.

2. Yet even these features are not impervious to the power of the imagination. For, to begin with, we often indulge in the converse exercise of considering what another person, e.g. one we admire, would do in the situation we find ourselves. In this case, it is exactly the "inner" features we just listed which need to be assumed, and the external circumstances kept as they are. But, of course, we can alter both domains to meet the challenge of understanding other human beings altogether: to see what "makes them tick", what makes them do the things they do, and so forth. This is an all-important task, for its result is likely to determine our attitude towards people; approval or condemnation, respect or contempt, sympathy or pity, they all depend on our representation of another being's inner life. And, as we have shown above, there is no way of representing a subject as such except by imagining being that subject. In attempting to do this, therefore, we

have to assume, to the best of our knowledge, all the circumstances and
all the attributes, inner and outer, of the person in question. Here the
issue is not what I would do in Carter's or Hitler's situation, but what
it must be like, for them, to be in that situation.

When you are reading about Hitler's last days in the bunker, you do
not fully meet the historian's challenge if you merely envisage the
dismal environment and the awful people; if you just survey with the
mind's eye the corridors, the cells, and the actors; if you just hear their
rantings and ravings between the explosions of the shells. What you also
have to do is to penetrate the minds of the participants: sense their
frustration and rage, as they contrast past glory and present misery;
conceive their false hopes based on wishful thinking, fanaticism, and
prejudice. Short of that, you do not really understand what is going on.
For those people, no matter how evil, are no mere automata, but
human beings with feelings and sentiments, memories and desires. And
if you do not understand them you cannot judge them, either. Because
to say that they were wicked men does not merely mean that they
wrought harm and destruction, for beasts and machines can do the
same, but rather that they did it knowingly: they did things which even
in their own eyes appeared wrong, or else those eyes had been distorted
in advance on purpose not to see. But then, to understand them, you
have to try to look at things through their eyes, corrupt as they are, in
much the same way as when you try to imagine the appearance of the
world to a colour-blind individual.

Now we realize the full importance of the possibility of transference.
In reading history, in enjoying a novel or a play, we encounter subjects
acting for reasons, and not merely objects causally determined to move
and to change. But a subject can be understood only subjectively: what
the senses reveal, and what science can trace, are but a challenge to the
imagination to do its work and represent that subject as an "I"; and the
only way of doing this is to imagine being that individual. If this is true
of characters in fiction and figures in history, it is also true of our
fellow men whom we encounter in daily life. It is only through the
possibility of transference that we are able to view other people and
animals as no mere automata but as creatures endowed with inner life:
this is how their movements and gestures, their frowns and smiles, the
expressions they show and the words they utter, are understood by us
as mere signs of what goes on in their minds, forever closed to our
senses, but open to our fancy. Without imagination, without the
possibility of transference, we all would be functional solipsists: we

could have no idea of another mind, or, for that matter, of any mind at all.

Thus, it appears, we are capable of transference; we are able to imagine being someone else. The question remains: how do we do it? What are the conditions warranting such a move? What is the "material", as it were, which we manipulate in imagination to achieve the end? And, finally, what are these "I"'s that we can shed and don at will as so many costumes, and what is this "I" that performs the change?

3. It is no doubt easier to imagine the inner life of another human being than that of a cat, and this, in turn, seems to be an easier task than imagining the "mind" of a rat, pigeon, bat, or crocodile. Why is this so?

The answer is quite simple. As we mentioned at the very beginning, we learn the use of "mental" predicates on the basis of external, mainly behavioural, indications. These marks, moreover, are primarily manifested in human behaviour, and only recognized in animals by a sort of analogy to human behaviour. An angry ape looks very much like an angry human, an angry rat much less, and I have no idea what an angry cockroach would look like. In addition, whereas humans can self-apply these predicates and thus confirm our surmises on their mental states, animals cannot, and consequently our judgments about their feelings and sentiments are bound to be less firm and far less specific. By and large one can recognize a sad dog (watch out with beagles, though), but hardly a nostalgic one.

We humans, at any rate, also learn to apply these predicates to ourselves without evidence. We learn how to describe our own sensations, feelings, and the like, to others by using the same expressions we learned to apply to other people. Now, obviously, we could not learn what to say, and when, if we could not recognize the external signs, on the basis of which we ascribe these predicates to other people, in our own physical set-up and behaviour. The child who cries because he stepped on a drawing-pin learns to say that his foot hurts, because he has observed that other people in similar circumstances, and he himself for that matter, are described in such terms. He also notices, however, that unlike such words as *tall, fat*, or *dirty*, expressions like *being in pain* are self-applied, with public acceptance, without the external manifestations. Soon he catches on, therefore, to the fact that being in pain does not consist in being in untoward physical circumstances, or in acting this way or that, but in having certain sensations which normally accompany the observable syndrome of stimulation and behaviour in his own experience.[1] Having got this far, he is able to use the term correctly. In saying, for example 'Daddy is in pain', when Daddy has been hurt, he will mean that Daddy feels what he would feel if he had been thus hurt. He will understand, moreover, what Mummy says when she complains of a headache, with or without external cause or other visible signs, since he knows what condition would prompt him to complain in like manner, even on occasions in which he would show no external signs.

He can easily do this with respect to Daddy, Mummy, and other humans, since their external susceptibility to stimulation, and the range of behavioural responses, are more or less the same as his own. In regard to cats, dogs, and the lesser endowed members of the animal kingdom, his imagination will be stretched more and more, till it breaks down in surmise and scepticism: do earthworms feel anything? Later on, when learning biology, he may be led to discover other analogies and differences between humans and animals, and thus to define the base of his empathy with the beasts more sharply, and increase his confidence in attributing or refusing elements of an inner life to them.

Thus we see that the very possibility of a learnable vocabulary of terms denoting features of an inner life depends upon the recognition of certain external syndromes in us and in others, which collectively form the "boundary conditions" for our imagination in the task of endowing beings with consciousness and subjectivity.

I do not want to suggest that the learning of a language is a necessary condition for the ability to recognize the manifestations of inner experience in others and in oneself. This cannot be, since deaf-mutes

[1] Contrary to some extreme interpretations of Wittgenstein, I maintain that we can speak of an association between a word and inner sensation. Granted, such an association cannot be established privately, but, once established, it forms the basis of the correct self-application of the word. It makes sense to say that we know what pain, tickle, etc., feel like. Accordingly we are able to represent to ourselves the condition of people telling the truth, or lying, about their inner experiences. For we can *imagine* what it is like to have a headache while denying it, and the other way around, or to see a pale face and make a compliment about rosy cheeks. And, to allay Wittgensteinian fears about the "private" nature of such associations, I remind you that "public" control remains: if anyone regularly claimed to be in pain in the absence of pain-producing stimuli and manifestations of pain, while using the word normally for other people, first he would be doubted, then his inconsistency pointed out; and if he used the word arbitrarily in both respects, he would be called silly, or ignorant of the meaning of the word. Thus the consistency required by the public use of these terms keeps their association with inner experience in proper alignment.

need not be solipsists. The point of my remarks is to show that the very possibility of the language we have depends upon the ability to perceive certain visible features as tokens of inner states. Children must be, therefore, natively equipped to put themselves in other beings' condition, and to view themselves objectively, as one among the others. Yet the learning of the language no doubt facilitates the development of this ability by helping the growth of an appropriate and refined conceptual repertory, in terms of which the conditions of these beings are perceived. This represents, in a subtle way, society's first contribution to individual development in this matter, even before the more intentional and explicit influences through training and instruction come to bear.

The native inclination to endow things with inner life explains why small children, and primitive people, are likely to sin by excess rather than defect in this matter: they consider dolls and trees as conscious beings, and are inclined to view nature as "full of gods". Development is likely to curb rather than encourage the original bent. As to the second aspect, viewing oneself objectively, the same small children and primitive people are inclined to refer to themselves as they do to others: by their names.

Hereby the first question posed at the end of the previous section has been answered: we attribute consciousness to ourselves and to others on the basis of certain observable conditions which we learned to associate with corresponding features of inner experience.

Before going on, just one more kick at the dead horse of the analogy-argument: if you say that I attribute consciousness to others because they are like me, I agree; but, I add 'also to myself, because I am like them'.

4. The question arises, however, how much these other beings are like me—not in their physical make-up, which is a relatively easy matter to establish, but in their inner life? What reason do I have to imagine, for instance, that they see red rather than, say, blue when they look at something red, and the other way round? Moreover, this traditional worry about the possibility of "inverted spectra" may be extended beyond the experiences of colour, or even beyond the visual domain altogether: perhaps some people feel tickle (often intolerably bad tickle) when burnt or cut, and pain when titillated on certain surfaces of their anatomy. 'But then they would tend to laugh when beaten . . . ' Not necessarily, I reply, since the subjective "qualia" (feelings of pain,

tickle, etc.) do not enter the causal chain (stimulus–brain state-behaviour) constituting the objective syndrome of being hurt, tickled, and so forth.[2] So, for example, the feeling of pain might accompany the entire syndrome of titilation. Remember Kripke's God from Chapter I: he could have paired physical states and inner experiences otherwise, either consistently throughout the domain of advanced organisms, or capriciously, thus creating such anomalies as inverted spectra, pain-tickle reversal, and the like. Notice, moreover, that once the flood-gates are open anything goes. As an extreme case, consider the idea of my present consciousness actually being attached to your current physical state, and vice versa.

This is absurd, of course, but why is it absurd? To find the answer let us return to the last sections of Chapter I. In a sweeping move we proceeded to endow all deserving organisms with inner life, i.e. we imagined what it would be like to be each one in turn. Needless to say we cannot, and we need not, complete this procedure: what really matters is the principle of transference, the existence of the "schema" of subjectivity for the imagination operating along the "second path". As a result we hit upon the self, i.e. the body whose projected experiences are open to my privileged access. This happy result, however, obviously hinges upon the consistent application of that schema. For otherwise I would not have any confidence in the outcome that I am indeed Z.V., and not somebody or something else. For if indeed anything goes in this matter, then I may be Jimmy Carter after all, since then his present physical state (that body in the Oval Office) might indeed register as the set of experiences I am having now (perception of a red pencil and of tankers going by). Worse, I may be one of those tankers themselves—or, why not, a disembodied spirit? For to say that anything goes is to say that I have no base to guide, no "boundary conditions" to limit, the flight of my fancy. Consequently the entire sense of the attempt to imagine what it must be like to be such and such is lost, and the whole enterprise cannot get off the ground.

I am bound, therefore, by the connections found in my experience between physical conditions and phenomenal content in endowing the deserving organisms with inner life, because only then will I emerge as the body to whose projected experiences I have a privileged access.[3]

---

[2] Thus my view, as the reader may have already gathered from Chapter I, amounts to epiphenomenalism. Toward the end of this work I shall defend my adherence to this much maligned position.

[3] I claimed above, against some interpreters of Wittgenstein, that it makes sense to speak of an association between public manifestations (and the words

5. This conclusion is still beset by two problems, the discussion of which will cast some new light on the nature of our whole argument.

The first is this. Let it be granted that I have to be consistent in assigning the features of inner life throughout the domain of higher organisms in my full, or "enriched", representation of the world, and that such a procedure is indispensable for my self-recognition within the same. Even so, there is no guarantee that things in fact conform to this representation: it still may be the case that the experiences of some sentient creatures are spectrum-reversed, pain-tickle inverted, or worse. For, to repeat, there is no way, ever, of peering into another mind to find out for sure; there is no way, in other words, to catch Kripke's God cheating.

My answer is as follows.[4] I deny that 'it still may be the case . . . ' We just agreed that I cannot be inconsistent in my assignment of the features of inner life and still hope to locate myself in the world. This means that no representation of the world in which I can recognize myself can allow for such a possibility. Compare this situation with imagining you with or without a hundred dollars in your pocket. I can do either of these things without doing any harm to my world-view as a whole. Consequently both states of affairs appear possible. Similarly, I can imagine you in Rome *or* Paris: both are possible. But I cannot put you in Rome *and* in Paris at the same time (say, talking to yourself long distance on the 'phone), for this would violate the transcendental conditions of representing individuals in the framework of space and time. And since the transcendental conditions governing the manifold of experience determine what is possible and what is not, it is impossible for you to be in those two places at once. Now, what I want to say is that the attribution of abberant "qualia" would violate the consistency requirement mentioned above, which is an equally transcendental condition of any representation of the world in which I can find myself. Hence it is impossible for you, or anybody, to experience inverted spectra and the like. Of course, I can still imagine

tied to them) on the one hand, and private experience on the other. Now it appears that without such a nexus one would have no means of representing another mind; one just would not have the colours to paint the picture. If, for instance, I did not know what pain feels like, I could not even begin to imagine what it must be like for somebody, anybody, being beaten, or twisted on the rack. And the same thing holds for all conditions which have a phenomenological counterpart. The whole possibility of transference, and hence of finding oneself in the world, depends upon this connection between observable syndrome and inner experience.

[4] Here I expand the lesson of the Parable of the Map-reader given in Chapter I.

you seeing red where I see blue, but in that case I have to assume that there is something deviant about your (or my) perceptual set-up (an easy way: coloured glasses); i.e. I have to tinker with the boundary conditions of my imaginative transference. To put it in general terms: the objective, physiological, conditions of sentient organisms determine their subjective experiences. Thus, for example, colour-blind individuals must be afflicted by a *physiological* defect. This relation, it appears now, is not due to identity, not even to a nomological nexus inductively discovered, but amounts to an a priori condition of representing conscious beings in the world. Thus Kripke's God is not all that powerful. But to see this, we first had to assume that he was.

6. The second problem arises as follows. I cannot even begin the imaginary enterprise of endowing some creatures with inner life if I do not know what sensory (and emotive) qualia correspond to what observable states. Now, since the only source of information I have in this respect is the relation of my mind (the only one to which I have a direct access) to my body, it seems to be the case that I must have identified myself (i.e. this body and this mind) *before* setting out to view some other beings as conscious too. If so, then one of the basic claims advanced in Chapter I is false, and the vaunted proof of other minds collapses into a variant of the analogy argument.

My answer is that this conclusion does not follow, because it is based on a confusion of psychological theory and philosophical justification. I have no definite idea of how *in fact* infants tie their experiences to their bodies. They certainly do, and they generally end up with a non-solipsistic representation of their little world, in which they find their places among the other creatures endowed with sensation, feeling, and thought. It is the psychologist's task to discover and to describe the steps the child goes through in arriving at this result. What I am interested in is the philosophical justification of the emerging view, in terms of which a sceptic about other minds may be answered. To use the terminology Kant adopted in a similar context, my concern is with the *quid iuris* and not the *quid facti* issue.

Consider two similar cases. The first is this. Let us assume that Hume was right about the ways in which humans acquire the notion of causality. His account, as is well known, amounts to a naturalistic, psychological theory. Such a theory, however, by no means preempts a philosophical defence of the objective notion of causality, such, for instance, as Kant's doctrine of the Second Analogy. What Kant tries to show is that no representation of a world in time is possible without an objective causal order. And this result is compatible with any psychological account of concept formation. In an exactly similar way, no physiological or psychological theory of perception is sufficient to provide a "refutation of idealism", which has to be achieved, if at all, by philosophical means.

Now, I view the problem of other minds in the same way. The psychological process of recognizing one's own body, and of acknowledging other minds in the world, has no bearing on the transcendental argument I gave in Chapter I, which demonstrates that the principle which *justifies* one's own self-recognition cannot be applied solipsistically; in other words, that there is no way of *accounting* for one's self-identity without attributing inner life to all deserving organisms.

Thus, there is no inconsistency in relying upon the connections found in one's own experience to provide the boundary conditions for the exercise of imagination leading to the recognition of one's own body and own self. What we are interested in is not *how we got the idea* of other minds, and of having a body, but in showing that *once we have got these ideas* we can justify them philosophically, and refute the sceptic by a transcendental argument based upon the very possibility of a self-containing world representation.

This defence can be made in another way, too. In order to be able to raise the philosophical problem of other minds, one must have certain notions in terms of which the problem can be posed. Concepts like "conscious", "sensation", "pain", and the like, must belong to this group. But we have argued that the logic of such "mental" notions shows a duality between objective marks (bodily states) and subjective experience. To put it bluntly, one knows what, say, being in pain is, only if one knows, first, what being in pain "looks" like, and second, what being in pain "is" like. If this second element is denied, then the problem cannot even arise. For, in that case, if you ask things like 'Are other people conscious?' or 'Is that cat in pain?' the answer would be 'Well, just look and see!' And such an answer, surely, is not the solution to the other minds problem.

But obviously the only way one can establish this connection between bodily state and quality of experience is via some incidents involving one's own body. This developmental fact, however, does not affect the content of the concept, since, as we saw, it is learned as applicable, in the same sense, to oneself and to others. The fact that

I learned a concept from a certain textbook does not belong to the concept . . .

Thus, although it is essential for the enterprise of showing the existence of other minds that we have these "combined" concepts, it is incidental how the combination is learned. Accordingly I do not have to presuppose that I am this man, to embark upon the task.

7. As we have seen above, in trying to understand other people we are often called upon not merely to "step into their shoes", as it were, by assuming some of their circumstances and attributes in imagination, but to perform a complete transference by imagining being another creature at some juncture of its life. We have expressed our confidence in the power of fancy, moreover, to carry out the task by exchanging as much in the content of our consciousness as proves to be necessary to represent the inner life of another being.

This confidence seems to be well founded. In principle, at least, there is nothing that could be experienced by me which I cannot represent in imagination. For one thing, I can imagine the wildest turns my life could have taken in the past or might yet take in the future. As to the present, too, I can imagine being in any situation my understanding can conceive: not only "wild" things again, such as walking on the other side of the moon, but things even more radical, such as being seven feet tall, blind, or perhaps, being sixteen years old again.

Nay, I can invent, and savour in my fancy, an entirely different life-history for me. One's past is like a line with uncountable potential nodes at which it might have forked in another direction. Let me select, then, a very early node in my life and pursue an alternative branch. Suppose that I have been stolen by gypsies in early infancy (after all, the scene is Hungary). I can imagine growing up in a covered wagon, learing to play the violin but not philosophy, being now a member of a band, respected grandfather to a bunch of little urchins, and so forth. Not even my appearance would be the same: I could be portly, with more hair on my head, and with a waxed mustache in the middle of my face.

Have I just imagined being a gypsy? 'Not quite,' you say, 'for it takes a gypsy to generate a gypsy, and you did not alter your pedigree.' But what difference does it make—I reply. If things were as I just imagined them, I would not know my real ancestry, and would believe myself to have been born within the tribe. And my memory would not contain anything incompatible with that belief: one does not remember one's birth and the first months of life. Therefore what I imagined could be indistinguishable from the mind of a gypsy of true blood. It follows, then, that the power of my imagination is sufficient to represent the mind of a real gypsy, and since I am not one, this shows that I can imagine being someone else. And that someone else may be anybody: one particular gypsy, you, Jimmy Carter, Napoleon, or what have you. All I have to do is observe an individual in its particular circumstances, or reconstrue a historical situation, say Napoleon at Waterloo, and then imagine being in the same situation myself, looking over the battlefield, seeing the Guards in their hopeless charge, hearing the drums beat and the canons roar, and so forth. This is not enough, of course, as we know, for I also have to try to assume Napoleon's mind with his memories, hopes, and desires, and the pain due to his well-known bodily affliction.

'But how do you know', you object, 'that you are right in your imagination? You are bound to be wrong, in some detail at least, in imagining what Napoleon *de facto* saw or heard, and even more so in recapturing his sentiments and thoughts. So you cannot succeed in imagining what it must have been really like for Napoleon to be at Waterloo.'

I reply by pointing out that, if this argument were correct, then one could prove along parallel lines that no one can draw or paint a picture of Napoleon, which is plainly false. No picture can capture all the details of its subject, and no picture will be true to life in all the details it represents. There are good and bad pictures of Napoleon, but even the best do not reproduce him entire, or without some distortion. In a similar way, I can, no doubt, imagine the Eiffel Tower now. Yet I could not vouch that I am right in every detail, or that my attention embraced all particulars.

What, then, makes a picture a picture of Napoleon? This is an old question, and I shall say more on it in due course. For the time being, I submit somewhat vaguely that, for example, a picture is a picture of Napoleon provided there is a causally linked series of representations connecting that picture with Napoleon himself. And what about my imagining the Eiffel Tower? In this case too, there has to be a causal chain between my idea of the Eiffel Tower, consisting of conceptual and sensory features preserved in memory, and that edifice itself. Thus I succeed in imagining the Eiffel Tower, albeit with greater or less accuracy, inasmuch as the work of my fancy is based on that well-connected idea.[5]

[5] Here, and in the subsequent discussion of this topic in Chapter IV, I rely upon some of Kaplan's views expressed in 'Quantifying In'.

The same thing holds about Napoleon. Only in this case, as we remember, my imagination can follow a double track: it is one thing, for instance, to imagine Napoleon on the field of Waterloo, and another to imagine being Napoleon on the field of Waterloo. The first task is similar to imagining the Eiffel Tower, but the second is not. Yet in either case, provided that my imaginative exercise is based on my well-connected idea of Napoleon, and on the circumstances of that battle known to me, it is Napoleon, his body, or his mind, that I imagine in those circumstances, regardless of the incompleteness and possible inaccuracy of detail.

Thus we see the answer to the second question posed above. The *materia ex qua* of transference is imagined experience; and since items of experience are not marked as mine or thine, a complex of experience may suffice to represent a given state of another mind, provided that the synthesis of that complex is based on a well-connected idea of the individual concerned, and on the knowledge of the circumstances involved.

8. There are well-known and much-discussed difficulties about seeing Napoleon, for instance, in a picture. And, obviously, there are even greater problems concerning seeing Napoleon, with the mind's eye, in imagination. All these troubles pale, however, in comparison with a fundamental problem besetting the task of imagining being Napoleon, or any other attempt at transference.

The difficulty arises as follows. In all the other cases, what one imagines is an actual or possible being, or state of affairs. If I imagine the Eiffel Tower, it is an actual construction that I fancy, and if I imagine the destruction of the Eiffel Tower, by terrorists for example, it is a possible state of affairs that I envisage in the imagination. The same holds about viewing Napoleon on the battlefield of Waterloo, following the battle, or even imagining a different course, with another outcome, for the same engagement. For it was possible for that battle to take another course. Similarly, when I imagined growing up and living among the gypsies, what I imagined was a very different, but still possible, sequence of experiences which I could have had if things had turned out otherwise.

But now consider the enterprise of imagining being Napoleon. This is not an objective exercise, like imagining the Eiffel Tower, or that battlefield, but a subjective one, similar in this respect to imagining growing up among the gypsies. Thus, I cannot keep my distance, as it

were, and look at things from the outside; it is a subject I have to represent, a being as an "I". I must put myself in an imaginary state, therefore, in which I can say that I am Napoleon. My being Napoleon is
what I have to imagine; this is the "state of affairs" that I have to
represent.

But, alas, I am not Napoleon. And, unfortunately for my attempted
transference, this is a necessary truth. All statements of identity (at
least between such "rigid designators" as names and indexicals), if
true, are necessarily true, and so are, accordingly, all statements of non-
identity. To speak in a fashionable idiom: there are possible worlds in
which Z.V. grows up among the gypsies, but there are none in which
he is born to Mr. and Mrs. Buonaparte in Ajaccio in the year 1769. Yet,
undoubtedly, I am Z.V., and this too seems to be a statement of
identity, and thus a necessary truth.[6]

Then the situation is clear. Necessarily, I am Z.V. Equally necessarily
Z.V. is not Napoleon. Hence, if I try to imagine being Napoleon, what
I try to imagine is something impossible; something, in other words,
that cannot be the case in any possible world.

What is left? An alternative: either I cannot imagine being Napoleon,
or, if I can, then I imagine something impossible in doing so. Unless, of
course, we are wrong in some of our assumptions . . .

9. Let us consider the first alternative in all generality. Transference is
impossible: I cannot really imagine being you, that cat, or Napoleon.
If I set out at all, I have to remain within the bounds of possibility.

I can still wonder, for instance, what it would be like, for me, to be
in Jimmy Carter's shoes—to be, that is, the President of the United
States. This kind of exercise does not cross identities, and what it
represents is a possible state of affairs; after all, if I can imagine a life
for me among the gypsies, I can imagine one leading me to the White
House. For one thing, I could even have been born in the U.S.A.—
if my mother had immigrated shortly before my birth.

We immediately realize, however, that this way out is a woefully
inadequate substitute for real transference. At the very beginning we
wondered about the cat, and tried to imagine what it must be like for
it to be in that sorry state. Now, Puss and Boots notwithstanding,
how on earth can I imagine myself being in its shoes? I am no cat,

---

[6] In this and the following paragraphs I follow Kripke's doctrine on identity
and individual essence, which to me seems to be intuitively correct. See his
Naming and Necessity.

I have no tail; there is no possible world in which the person who I am is born as a cat.

Then, what about Napoleon? The situation is equally bad: I, the off-spring of my parents, could not have been born in the eighteenth century, and by no stretch of the imagination can I fancy a life for me in which I would play a role in the aftermath of the French Revolution.

Nor could I imagine, within the bounds of the possible, what it must have been like growing up in the sixties, in this. country, among the turmoils of the Vietnam War. For I, Z.V., could not have been born even a year later than I was. The line of life has many potential branches, we observed above; but it has only one beginning. I may wonder what might have happened to me—once this "me" is given; but take away my origin, and nothing is left to wonder about.

It seems, then, that even the half-way house described above is barred, for the most part, by our present restrictions. As soon as you start saying things like 'If I had been in Hitler's situation in 1940 ...' I could cut in: 'But you could not have—you were two years old at that time.'

Needless to say, the task of understanding people we outlined above would be impossible altogether. Since I am not a Negro, I could not imagine what it must be like growing up and living as one in our society, or in South Africa; since I do not live in the Middle Ages, I could not try to capture the mind of a medieval monk, and so forth. And Robert Graves could not have written *I Claudius*.

But perhaps we misunderstand the task. Maybe we can do all these things on a less ambitious basis. 'What it must be like', we say, 'to be such and such.' And one thing may be *like* another without being the same. So instead of aiming at the impossible by trying to transcend the limitations of time and identity, we should be satisfied with imagin-ing being in a situation sufficiently similar to that of the object of our concern.

In replying to this suggestion, I wish to remark, first, that the use of the phrase *this is what x is (looks, feels, etc.) like* does not imply that the experience to which *this* refers is not the experience of a real *x*. On the contrary. Consider the following contexts: 'So this is what a supertanker looks like', said while looking at one of those monsters; 'This is what weightlessness feels like', uttered in the dropping heli-copter; 'Now if this is what being married is like, then I should have remained single'; and so forth. Accordingly, in trying to imagine what a supertanker must look like, the subject should try to imagine a supertanker, and not just something similar to a supertanker. And the bachelor who tries to imagine what it must be like to be married falls short in his enterprise if what he imagines is not the real thing but a mere substitute: cohabitation, engagement, or what have you. By the same token, finally, the person who tries to imagine what it must be like to be a cat, or Napoleon at the battle of Waterloo, should aim at representing these things, and not something else, in his mind.

'But if these things are impossible,' you insist, 'then he has to settle for the next best thing, to wit, imagining himself in a situation similar to that of the object of his interest.'

'This won't do,' I answer, and for a fundamental reason, which we seemed to have forgotten throughout this last discussion. The point of transference is supposed to be the representation of *another* mind, not my own in various possible circumstances. If I am not to remain alone in this world, I have to recognize other bodies as bodies of conscious beings, and the only way of giving content to the idea of another mind is to imagine being someone else. We ought to remember, moreover, that there is no way of representing my body as mine without endowing it with consciousness, and this for reasons which equally apply to other bodies. For how can I imagine what it must be like for me to live like a gypsy, for instance, if I do not imagine this body of mine in those circumstances first? But there are other bodies in similar circumstances—and the this and the that cannot make a difference.

We have to reject, then, the first alternative. The possibility of transference cannot be given up short of being doomed to solipsism, or rather being satisfied with a mechanistic universe with no place in it for *me*.

10. Thus we are driven to explore the other horn of the dilemma: in performing transference we can, and we do, imagine something impossible.

This is not a matter of fancying something merely false, something which just happens not to be the case. For that is an easy matter indeed: the faculty of imagination is tolerant enough to embrace truth and falsity with equal ease. I can imagine the Houses of Parliament with or without Big Ben, Napoleon winning at Waterloo, and, just a while ago, I imagined living in a covered wagon myself. Fiction, in general, is the daughter of fancy.

The impossible, however, is quite another thing. In ordinary matters —which are not the preserve of mathematicians, logicians, or practitioners of remote branches of physics—we regard the imagination as the arbiter of possibility. As the senses are trusted to show what is the case and what is not, so the imagination is supposed to reveal what is possible and what is not. Can you take off your shirt without removing your jacket? Confronted with this problem one does not reason with concepts—be they the concepts of those garments or notions of topology—but one tries to imagine executing the move, and the failure in the imaginary task is enough to show the impossibility of the real one.

There are, of course, all sorts of possibility: moral, scientific, and metaphysical. But the imagination nicely follows suit by representing what can and what cannot occur, in the course of normal human interaction, within the framework of reputable science, or just absolutely in a magic world in which even the laws of science are relaxed. For we can imagine miracles, and the exploits of Superman. Science may overrule the spontaneous verdict of the imagination here and there: think of Moebius-bands, twins whose ages differ owing to some really fast space-travel, and so forth. But even in these cases the imagination is merely stalled and not defeated; it may be slow to follow the understanding, but does not remain in permanent conflict with it.

In matters of identity too, the imagination seems to remain a reliable guide to what is possible. I could have grown up among the gypsies without the slightest harm to my identity, since I can imagine a sequence of events, beginning with my birth, which amounts to this possibility. And so can I imagine Napoleon's life to be quite different from what it was in actuality. He might have remained on Corsica and become a schoolteacher; or, more probably, a highwayman; or, again, he might have died of smallpox at the age of four. In all these speculations I keep *him* in mind: that child, born to those parents, who is known to us through the role he actually played in history. To this restriction I have to adhere, so long as it is Napoleon I am thinking about. Thus, I cannot imagine *him* to have been born, say, in the thirteenth century. Why not? Because no child born in that age would have the same range of possible lives that awaited the baby Napoleon, consequently my imagination would not merely run through the various branches of the same tree, but would represent another tree altogether.

Leibniz's law governs identity and difference, provided that it is interpreted in a non-Leibnizian fashion: the description of each individual, each "individual concept" in his terms, should include not merely its actual history, but all possible histories as well.[7] But what makes those histories histories of the same individual? The common point

[7] For Leibniz's views see mainly his *Correspondence with Arnauld*.

they all share, I answer, namely, the insertion of that individual, with
its native endowment, into the fabric of the universe at a particular
point of time and circumstance. This view, as I explained elsewhere,
is in accordance with common sense in two basic respects.[8] First, it
allows us to claim, contrary to Leibniz, that the very same individual,
Adam, Napoleon, or I, could have lived different lives and yet remained
the same person. And second, it accounts for the importance of origin
for each individual: once this is given, we have a subject to speculate
about; without it, we cannot even begin.

Thus, we cannot imagine Napoleon living in the Middle Ages or
being Robespierre. In a similar way, although we can imagine the
Mississippi with a somewhat altered course, we cannot imagine it being
the Danube; we can imagine the moon more pockmarked than it is, or
following a different orbit, but we cannot imagine it to be the same
body as the sun; and so forth.

Nor can I imagine, so it appears now, Z.V. being Napoleon, or anybody else for that matter. Even if I fancy a life for me approximating
to that of Napoleon, it will be one of *my* possible lives and not his:
our origins are distinct, and that gap cannot be bridged by the mightiest
efforts of that formidable faculty.

How is it, then, that I took it for granted up to now, with what I
thought to be the full sanction of common sense, that I can imagine
being Napoleon? Yet I, surely, am Z.V.—who else?

We seem to be thoroughly confused. Both our alternatives fell to the
ground: we must be able to imagine being somebody else, we concluded
in the previous section; we cannot possibly imagine being somebody
else, we demonstrated in this.

11. It is time to let Reason speak, and she begins as follows: 'The
whole trouble arises from the fact that you represented transference in
a wrong way from the outset; no wonder it appears as an impossible
task. Let us consider your own example, Napoleon. Of course, I can
imagine being Napoleon; but to do so I do not have to imagine *myself*
being him. That, as you correctly pointed out, is an impossibility, both
for fact and for fancy. Fortunately, however, all I have to do is imagine
being Napoleon. Nothing is said about me. And, of course, being
Napoleon is a perfectly possible state, since, for one thing, Napoleon
himself was in it. So it is not merely a possible but an actual state, *de
facto* occurring in the universe. True, it is a subjective state, but we at

[8] In 'On the Possibility of Possible Worlds'.

least have no quarrel with the reality of subjective things. As you can imagine other things in the world, e.g. the Eiffel Tower, the battle of Waterloo, the taste of coffee, or being married, you can imagine being Napoleon. Why not? One more thing, which you yourself mentioned a while ago, but seem to have forgotten since. If I imagine being Napoleon, and you imagine being Napoleon, we imagine the same thing. And, obviously, this could not be so if what you imagined were your being Napoleon, and if what I imagined were my being Napoleon. As a matter of fact, however, what you and I both imagine is being Napoleon pure and simple, without you's and me's. Once more, it is like with the Eiffel Tower or similar things. We both can imagine it, and what we imagine is the same thing: that tower and nothing else.'

Thus spake Reason, and I am duly impressed. As the Voice of Reason reminds me, my being Z.V. rather than, say, Napoleon, does not make any difference in the world: not in the physical universe, which contains our bodies at diverse locations in space and time, and not in the "enriched" universe we projected by endowing all deserving bodies with consciousness, including Napoleon's and mine. Consequently, if I imagine being Napoleon, I do not imagine things otherwise than they are. Thus, I am not at all committed to envisage the false, nay, impossible, state of affairs in which Vendler and Napoleon are the same, with their bodies and minds confused. Vendler remains Vendler, and Napoleon Napoleon. But, in addition to remaining content with being Vendler in actual experience, I can indulge, now and then, in being Napoleon, or anybody I fancy, vicariously in imagination. To say this, however, is not to belittle this ability; what we said above about the importance of this move remains valid: without it we could not represent other minds, as contrasted with our own, at all.

Let us put it this way: I am actually "hooked" to the universe by the mind and body of Z.V.: this is "where" I find myself. But this bond can be overcome by the force of imagination: I can imagine being anchored elsewhere, via another mind and body. This is the fulfilment of the demand made at the end of the first chapter: 'To represent another as oneself, and oneself as another.'

Nevertheless, a gnawing worry remains. Since I am Vendler and not Napoleon, in imagining being Napoleon I still seem to represent things otherwise than as they are. What things? Nothing in the world, to be sure. It is not like imagining the Eiffel Tower pink. That, if you like, is imagining a different possible world. But imagining being Napoleon is not. Thus the fact, if it is to be called a fact, that I am Z.V., and the fact that I am not Napoleon, are not facts that "belong" to the description of the universe.[9] Yet nothing is more obvious to me than that I am this man and not that. My puzzlement comes down to this: I understand what Z.V. is, but I still do not understand what this "I" is that happens to be Z.V., yet in such a way that it can imagine being someone else without imagining anything which is not so in the world. What sort of thing is this "I", and what do I say when I assert 'I am Z.V.'? And, finally, what is the nature of this all powerful force, the faculty of imagination, that seems to belong to that "I"?

To speak of a Transcendental Self is to disturb a hornet's nest at once. It will be safer, and more profitable as we shall see, to examine first the faculty of imagination, which we all have, and, I hope, all admit to having.

[9] This distinction is noticed in Lewis's paper, 'Attitudes De Dicto and De Se'.

III

Vicarious Experience

1. WE ARE looking down upon the ocean from a cliff. The water is rough and cold, yet there are some swimmers riding the waves. 'Just imagine swimming in that water' says my friend, and I know what to do. 'Brr!', I say as I imagine the cold, the salty taste, the tug of the current, and so forth. Had he said 'Just imagine yourself swimming in that water', I could comply in another way, too: by picturing myself being tossed about, a scrawny body bobbing up and down in the foamy waste. In this case I do not have to leave the cliff in imagination: I may see myself, if I so choose, from the very same perspective. Not so in the previous case: if I indeed imagine being in the water, then I may see the cliff above me, but not myself from it.

I shall call the act of imagination involved in the first exercise subjective, and the one in the second objective. As the swimming example shows, the second kind consists in the inner representation of one's body (or voice) from a certain perspective. This task is no different from the representation of other bodies; after all, I can imagine you floating in the ocean with equal ease. The other kind does not call for the representation of my body from a distinct point of view; it merely consists in evoking the experiences I would have if I were in some situation or other. To put it in another way: in the objective case I fancy seeing (or hearing) what *I* would look (or sound) like in a given situation, whereas in the subjective case I fancy experiencing what *it* would be like to be in such a situation.

In order to familiarize yourselves with this distinction, imagine eating a lemon (sour taste), and them imagine yourself eating a lemon (pinched face); imagine being on the rack (agony), and then yourself being on the rack (distorted limbs); imagine whistling in dark (sensation of puckered lips), and then yourself whistling in the dark (distance uncertain, but coming closer); and so forth.

2. Consider once more the two injunctions we mentioned at the beginning:

> (1) Imagine swimming in that water
> (2) Imagine yourself swimming in that water

I have suggested that (1) demands the subjective reading, but (2) requires, or at least permits, the objective. Yet the two sentences differ only in the word *yourself*. Moreover, one might argue, this difference is no difference, since the verb-complements in both (1) and (2) are derived from the same sentence in the deep-structure, to wit:

> (3) You (are) swim(ming) in that water

This suggestion is supported by the intuition that in both cases it is the subject's own swimming that is the object of his imagination. This is obvious in (2), since the reflexive marker, *self*, is affixed to *you*, which indicates the identity of the imaginer and the swimmer. It is true, of course, that *you*, the subject of *imagine*, is missing from (2), but this is a standard feature of the imperative; think of *Shave yourself!* Notice, moreover, that even *yourself* can be omitted without much loss: *Shave!* normally means shave yourself. So it is possible to argue that in (1) too, not only the *you* before *imagine*, but *yourself* after *imagine*, are omitted on the surface. This line of argument is strengthened by the fact that in the sentence,

> Imagine shaving yourself

the *self* indicates the suppressed presence of *you* as the subject of *shave*. For that *self* cannot reflect the *you* belonging to *imagine*, because in that case the following sentence would be grammatical:

> *Imagine him shaving yourself

Which it is not. (NB: the asterisk marks deviant sentences.)

Yet these arguments cannot be right. (1) and (2) do require (or allow for) different readings; therefore, if linguists are right, they cannot have the same underlying structure. And this can be shown by a more obvious proof as well. *Imagine* in (2) can be replaced by the verb *picture* without loss of meaning or grammaticality:

> Picture yourself swimming in that water

A similar substituion spoils (1):

*Picture swimming in that water

It follows, therefore, that the two verb-complements:

> . . . swimming in that water

> . . . yourself swimming in that water

have different verb-demands; consequently, the verb *imagine* must figure differently in (1) and (2). And, of course, it does: as we explained before, (2) calls for an objective representation, a *picturing* in this particular case, but (1) does not.

3. It seems, therefore, that (3) correctly represents the source of *yourself swimming in that water* in (2). This accounts for the fact that the subject of *swim* can be raised out of similar sentences in such emphatic forms as

> It is myself (and not you) that I imagined swimming in that water

Sentences like (1), on the other hand, yield the following emphatic version:

> It is swimming (and not wading) that I imagined doing in that water

The emergence of *do* after *imagine* is very revealing. In complying with (1) you imagine doing something, in complying with (2) you imagine yourself (or, in other cases, somebody else) doing something.

In the light of this difference, it is not too difficult to account for the structure of (1). There are groups of aspectual verbs that show the same behaviour as the subjective *imagine*. I have in mind *start, stop, continue*, and *resume* on the one hand, and *appear* and *seem* on the other. Consider the following sentences:

> He started running
> He resumed talking to the crowd
> She appeared to be floating over the water

and so forth. Then notice that these verbs also behave like the subjective *imagine*, when followed by a reflexive construction:

> He started shaving himself
> She appeared to be hitting herself

Obviously, the subject of *shave* is *he*, and the subject of *hit* is *she*, notwithstanding the intervening aspectual verbs, *start* and *appear*. Even the emphatic forms follow suit nicely:

> It is shaving himself that he started doing
> It is hitting herself that she appeared to be doing

Let us assume, then, that the verb *imagine*, at least sometimes functions as an aspectual verb. Accordingly, the subject of *swim* in (1) is *you*, and the verb *imagine* is nothing but an aspectual modifier of *swim*. In the following discussion I am going to show that this hypothesis is an illuminating and fertile one.

4. First of all, inspired by the spirit of Ockham's famous dictum, we may ask the question whether there are indeed two senses of the verb *imagine*, i.e. the subjective and the objective, or whether we can get by with the subjective one alone, with which we just have learned to cope. Is there a way, in other words, to reduce objective occurrences to subjective ones?

Compare, once more, (1) and (2). How can we derive something like (2) from something like (1)? Well, what exactly does (1) call for? Above, we said this: it calls for 'evoking the experiences I would have if I were in a certain situation', in the water in that case. What are these experiences? We mentioned feeling cold, tasting salt, and seeing the cliff above. This last one holds the key to the magic box. Because, unquestionably, imagining being in some situation or other involves not merely fancying tactual, muscular, or kinaesthetic sensations, but auditory and visual ones as well. Consequently, imagining myself swimming in that water, or imagining you running on the field, can be understood in terms of imagining seeing myself swimming in that water, and imagining seeing you running in the field. And what about imagining you (or myself) whistling in the dark? Obviously, what this means is imagining hearing you (or myself) whistling in the dark. If this is true, then (2) is nothing but an elliptical product of

> Imagine seeing yourself swimming in that water

Seeing simply drops out by the familiar process of removing redundancy.

In some cases, however, the deletion of the perceptual verb might lead to ambiguity, which may be resolved by supplying the omitted verb. Suppose you tell me 'Imagine Rubinstein playing this piece.'

'Yes, I see him sitting straight, his fingers running over the keyboard.'
'No, that is not what I mean; imagine hearing him play it on the radio.'

Deletions of the same kind often occur with some of the other aspectual verbs mentioned above. For example:

> Tolstoi started *War and Peace* in 1865
> The gang finished the road two weeks ago

It is clear that what Tolstoi started was *writing War and Peace*, and what the gang did was to finish *building* the road. Even ambiguities can occur, for the same reason as with *imagine*. If I say

> I started *War and Peace* two weeks ago

people who are familiar with literature will understand that, unlike Tolstoi, I started reading, and not writing, *War and Peace*.

The suppressed presence of the perceptual verb (mainly *see* or *hear*) can also be demonstrated by the adverbs such sentences can take. Consider the following examples:

> Imagine the battlefield from above
> Imagine this statue sideways
> Imagine the music coming from a distance

It is clear that what is meant here is seeing the battlefield from above, the statue from the side, and hearing the music coming from a distance. For, if these adverbs were to modify the verb *imagine* itself, rather than the deleted perceptual verbs, then nothing would prevent the formation of such sentences as

> *Imagine a thunderbolt from the side
> *Imagine the taste of lemons from above

The verb *imagine* can indeed take adverbs on its own. The most notable one is *vividly*. And, notice, *vividly* does go with *imagine* regardless of the kind of perception involved. One can imagine vividly the battlefield, the thunderbolt, the taste of lemons, and what not.

It is particularly important to realize that the element of perspective involved in visual and auditory fantasy is due to the perspective nature of vision, and, to a lesser extent, of hearing. These senses, unlike, say, taste and smell, are eminently "objective" in the etymological sense of the word: they put the perceiver in a spatial relation to the object. Hence one can see, and imagine seeing, a lion *coming* towards one, the building *towering above* one, and one can hear, and imagine hearing, church-bells *far-away*, the sound of the train *coming close*, or *fading away in the distance*.

It will be objected that the verb *picture*, which we could substitute for *imagine* in (2), does not tolerate the addition of a perceptual verb. We do not have, for instance,

　　　*Picture seeing John in the water

This fact can be explained by the assumption that this use of *picture* simply amounts to *imagine seeing*. If so, then it is not surprising to find that *picture* is out of place with auditory fantasy, e.g.

　　　*Picture a thunderbolt

and with the subjective imagining of (1):

　　　*Picture swimming in that water

Picture, therefore, is a real verb, albeit with an aspectual element included. The same thing is true of a related verb: *visualize*. Not so *fancy*. It is a near synonym to *imagine*, as can be shown by the possibility of such sentences as

　　　Just fancy driving that car
　　　Fancy hearing Caruso singing that aria

We may illustrate the derivation of (1) and (2) by means of Figures 1 and 2.

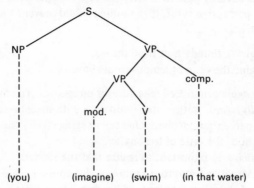

Figure 1.

5. Finally, one might ask the question whether it is indeed *see*, rather than *look at*, which is the perceptual verb deleted from the sentences

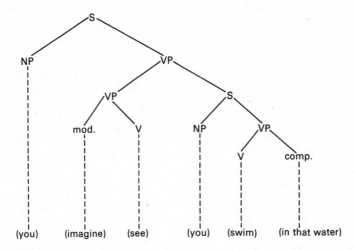

Figure 2.

calling for or reporting feats of visual imagination. By using the appropriate adverb test, we can show that *look at* would hardly fit. Typical adverbs of *look at* are *intently, carefully, from left to right*, and the like. Indeed, one can imagine looking at the Escorial intently, carefully, and from left to right. Nothing surprising in this, since looking, like swimming and shaving, is an action one can imagine doing. The point is, however, that the adverbs alone will not do; the sentences

Imagine the Escorial intently
Imagine the battlefield from left to right

are marginal at best. Thus, whereas there is nothing wrong with imagining the Escorial from above, since one can see the Escorial from above, there is something funny about imagining the Escorial from left to right, because there is something funny about seeing the Escorial from left to right. It appears, then, that *imagining the Escorial* comes from *imagining seeing the Escorial* rather than *imagining looking at the Escorial*.

There are some other adverbial phrases, however, which although compatible with *see* would not stand up with *imagine* alone. One can see things in a mirror, through binoculars, and out of the corner of one's eye. Yet again, such sentences as

> Imagine the Eiffel Tower through binoculars
> I just imagined the Escorial out of the corner of my eye

are seriously deficient. Why is this so?

The answer seems to be that these adverbs, no less than the previous group, are primarily adverbs of *looking*, and not of *seeing*. What they describe is the physical mode of perceiving rather than the experiential content of perception. Compare, for instance, *from above* and *in a mirror*. The qualification *seen from above* selects a definite aspect or perspective of the object perceived; *seen in the mirror*, on the other hand, says something about the way the perceiver goes about looking at the object, which is compatible with any aspect perceived.

Looking at something—as much as watching, observing, viewing, contemplating, and the like—is a bodily action or state, and as such publicly observable, depictable, and objectively imaginable. Seeing or perceiving something is not. I can catch you looking at a pornographic picture; Rembrandt painted Aristotle contemplating Homer's bust; and you can imagine me, or yourself, staring at the moon. But can I ever catch you seeing anything? Could Rembrandt's painting be called *Aristotle seeing Homer's bust*? And can you, finally, imagine me perceiving the moon?

We know, of course, that—unlike seeing—watching, looking at, observing, and the rest, are actions we can do deliberately and carefully, with or without such auxillary instruments as mirrors and telescopes. And, as with any other actions, I can imagine doing these actions too: for example, observing the moon. through a telescope. The point is, however, that I can imagine seeing something without these paraphernalia; I can imagine the pure experience of perceiving the moon without dragging instruments, my eyes, or my body, into the imaginary exercise. In trying to imagine seeing a landscape on the other side of the moon I do not have to worry about my poor body in that inhospitable environment. For the same reason, in imagining (seeing) myself crossing the street, I do not have to duplicate my body. What I conjure up in this case is simply the visual experience of seeing Vendler crossing the street, and not the experiences *of Vendler* observing Vendler crossing the street.

The boot, in fact, is on the other foot. In trying to imagine *observing* a landscape on the other side of the moon, I do have to fancy being bodily there. And this exercise will consist in putting together an appropriate cluster of visual, tactual, kinaesthetic and other experiences in imagination, corresponding to my idea of the circumstances that would affect my body in those surroundings.

Thus it seems that Philonous was at least partly right in Berkeley's famed dialogue.[1] Although one can imagine a tree unobserved, one cannot imagine it unseen. For to imagine a tree is to imagine seeing it, but this does not mean that an observer too has to be added to the scene. And, of course, one can understand the idea of a tree unseen or unobserved.

To conclude: the *materia ex qua* of all imagination is imagined experience: sights and sounds—not as physical things, but as pure perceptions—and other sensations, feelings and sentiments; those subjective things, in other words, with which we learned to cope in Chapter I. These are the atoms out of which the world of the imagination, subjective and objective, is constructed.

6. The fact that the verb *imagine* is but an aspectual modal in such contexts also explains its curious behaviour with respect to time-determination. The first peculiarity that strikes the eye is the almost complete absence of progressive tenses in its use. I certainly can imagine crossing a wide avenue, and such a crossing takes a considerable amount of time. One would expect, therefore, that imagining crossing that avenue would also go on in time, and in fact take a comparable length of time. Yet it is somewhat odd to say things like "I am now imagining crossing a wide avenue," or for that matter, "I was imagining Sir Edmund Hilary climbing the final peak of Mount Everest for five minutes". Moreover, whereas I can imagine crossing the avenue slowly or fast, it does not follow that the latter feat involves some fast bit of imagining, taking a shorter time than the former. The act of imagination, which no doubt occurs in real time, brackets the process represented in its own temporal framework, which is not synchronized with current experience, much in the same way as the perspective of a picture is not integrated into its physical environment, notwithstanding the fact that the picture itself is located in real space.

Compare, for instance, observing somebody crossing the street, and imagining somebody crossing the street. In the first case, there are two processess running concurrently in real time: the crossing and the observing. In the second case, however, the crossing is an imagined process, which is not to be fitted into real time; thus it cannot impose any definite duration on the act of imagining it, which does occur

[1] *First Dialogue between Hylas and Philonous.*

in real time. There is no more reason to think that imagining a longer process than a shorter one should take longer time than to think that the
picture of an elephant should cover more paper than a picture of a mouse.

Yet, just as all pictures take up some surface, acts of imagining doing
things, too, are likely to need some real time. This point may account
for such notorious exercises as counting sheep on a sleepless night. Even
there, though, no real matching could be established between the
duration of the imagined sequence and the time consumed in projecting
it in our fancy.

Finally, to anticipate: the same independence of duration is the
mark of other forms of vicarious experience: a "long" dream may occur
in a short sleep, and it does not require a long time to recall a pro-
longed agony in the dentist's chair.

7. What can you imagine? I shall start with considering the feats of
imagination which we called subjective. These, as we remember, consist
in imagining doing something or being in some situation or condition:
we mentioned swimming, walking, looking at something, living in a
covered wagon, and so forth. Will any action or condition do? Obviously
not. One cannot imagine being dead, sound asleep, or breathing while
sound asleep. Nor can one imagine growing, or digesting food, unless
one fancies certain experiences that might be indicative of such processes. Needless to say, one can imagine some person or organism being
dead, sound asleep, or digesting food, but that would not be a subjective exercise.

Can one imagine having purple eyes? Not directly; the closest one
can get to it is imagining seeing oneself in the mirror with purple eyes.
What about imagining being tall? This is much easier, since being tall
has all sorts of consequences for the quality of one's experience: looking down on other people, seeing better in the cinema, and the like.

What all those examples show is that the necessary condition for
imagining performing certain actions, or being in certain conditions,
is the experiential content attached to these things. It must make
sense, in other words, to ask the question: what would it be like doing
such a thing or being in such a state? One can imagine being dead only
if one assumes, falsely I think, that being dead is compatible with, and
is characterizable by, having certain experiences. Thus it is possible
to imagine being blind, deaf, dumb, etc., but not being without any
perceptions at all, which would be required to imagining being really
dead or sound asleep.

There is one domain remaining: epistemic states. Ask the question: what is it like to think or to believe that something is the case; to remember that something has occurred, or to expect that something will? What would it be like to believe, for instance, that the earth is flat; or to expect the Second Coming soon? If these things are like anything, then I should be able to fancy being in such mental states. I do not think that they are directly: beliefs, expectations, and the like, are not experiences, consequently *per se* do not belong to the domain of fantasy. But remember fancying being tall by imagining some of the experiences such a state would bring about. Then think of the mind of a believer in a flat earth. Does he merely say to himself and to others 'The earth is flat, the earth is flat'? No, if he is sincere in his belief, then he will represent to himself the earth as a flat disk, suspended in space, or floating on waters. And these and similar things are perfectly imaginable. Thus, by imagining the earth to be such, by imagining journeys to the edge of the earth and looking down, etc., I imagine, to some extent at least, what it would be like believing that the earth is flat. Far be it from me to suggest that a belief is nothing but a certain pattern of imagination, or a disposition to act in a certain way. Nevertheless it is these patterns of fancy and behaviour that manifest a belief in one's own experience; it is by these means that it is like something, for an individual, to have a belief. And since these things are imaginable, nothing that constitutes the actual awareness of a mind, no matter how exotic in its beliefs, is impervious to the force of the imagination.

Thus we reach the limit of the power of subjective imagination: imagining being somebody or something else altogether, i.e. performing transference. Another mind, at a certain moment of its history, is a complex of experiences, feelings, memories, beliefs, and expectations. And, as we just saw, none of these things are beyond the power of subjective imagination. So I can imagine being a king, a beggar, a cripple, a child, or a cat; or try to do so, at least, without absurdity. Also, in reading history or fiction, we find ourselves imagining being Caesar, Napoleon, Hamlet, or even being Napoleon at the battle of Waterloo. In these cases, of course, as we mentioned above and shall see in more detail later on, there has to be a link connecting our notion of these individuals to those persons, real or fictional, to assure that it is *their* minds that we represent in our fancy.

8. It has been suggested above that the raw material for the constructions of fantasy are imagined experiences. The question arises how

these experiences are related to the real ones? In other words, what is the phenomenological equivalent of the linguistic modality marked by the verbs *imagine* and *fancy*?

The first and most obvious fact is the independence of one's imagination from the concurrent condition of one's body, and the actual perceptions one may have. We can "see" with the mind's eye while the bodily ones are closed or otherwise occupied. Beethoven could "hear" the Ninth Symphony his deafness notwithstanding, and the fantasy of sumptuous meals is often triggered by the pangs of an empty stomach.

Nevertheless, the actual exercise of the bodily senses often interferes with the exercise of the imagination. One is likely to close one's eyes to allow the mind's eye to do its job, and it is quite hard to imagine hearing a Chopin nocturne while being exposed to a blast of hard rock. Also, perception and fantasy can work hand in hand on the same material: think of such situations as holding a picture in one's hand and staring at the wall to "see" where it would look best; wondering how the dress one sees in the shop-window would look on one's wife, and so forth. Common experience further shows that vivid imaginings are able to produce the same psychological or even physiological reactions as their real counterparts. Imagining eating tasty food, or lemons, stimulates salivation, and the lecher's dirty mind is aimed at provoking actual *delectatio morosa*. It seems, therefore, that from a phenomenological point of view there is an affinity between real experiences and imaginary ones. It is reasonable to assume, moreover, that at least the same functions of the central nervous system are being activated in either case: by sensory input in the one, and by some inner stimulus, or sheer "will," whatever it is, in the other.

Yet, in spite of the independence from bodily conditions, the play of the imagination is not entirely voluntary. St. Anthony in the desert could testify to this point. Nevertheless the power of the will enjoys a certain immediacy with respect to the content of fancy, which it lacks in regard to real experiences. One cannot even hope to change one's experiences without first disposing one's body otherwise: moving away from the fire, scratching the itch, or closing one's eyes. Not so with imagined experiences. Although they often arise unasked for, and are reluctant to disappear, whatever control the will does have is exercised directly, and not merely through its conscious power over the members of the body. One is able to put aside, as it were, the haunting images that prevent sleep, and count sheep instead, without moving a limb or batting an eye.

These two features, independence from bodily conditions, and direct control by the will, lead to another mark, already discussed a short while ago. We have found that one can imagine seeing the Escorial without imagining looking at it in the body, seeing a lion in the mind's eye without fancying confronting one in the flesh, and so forth. Similarly, I can imagine hearing the Ninth Symphony without putting myself in a concert-hall, in front of a radio, or the like, in fantasy. To put it in general terms: one can imagine isolated experiences, elements of a consciousness, without reproducing its totality, in much the same way as one can draw a lion, or even a lion's head, without its visible environment, its roar, or smell. Speaking of lions: imagining seeing a lion does not trigger fear—one is not "there", not even in fantasy; imagining facing a lion is another matter indeed—it provokes fear, perhaps even a shiver in one's back. Real experience is given in totality, and the role of the will is restricted to guiding the attention to single details; imaginary experience is built up from its elements, and its completion is the result of an interplay of will, associations, and, of course, the transcendental conditions of possible experience.

9. The phenomenological, and perhaps organic, kinship of experience and fantasy also explains the origin of our imaginative repertory. We can imagine being in pain because we have felt pain in the past, and I can imagine the Escorial green because I am not colour-blind. But, if one has never had them, one cannot imagine such "exotic" experiences as drug-induced hallucination, mystical trance, or simple weightlessness. Still less can we imagine the sonar-perceptions enjoyed by bats, or the sensitivity to geomagnetic forces some migratory birds may possess.

Do such shortcomings imply that therefore I cannot imagine being St. Teresa of Avila, or that bat flapping about in the garden? Not at all. Think of a man natively blind. He, presumably, had no experience of colour, therefore he cannot imagine what red flags and blue dresses look like. Can he imagine being me, or some other sighted individual? Of course he can; Helen Keller was no solipsist. We only have to recall what we said above about the pictures of Napoleon: there are black-and-white pictures of Napoleon, yet he surely was not black-and-white. As a simple line-drawing can be a picture of Napoleon, provided the pedigree of that picture is authentic, so my representation of Saint Teresa's mind, or of that bat's consciousness, will do, if my ideas of these subjects are derived from them. For there are many features that can fill out these representations; even that bat is a mammal, after all, something like a mouse, enjoying food, rest and exercise, suffering pain and hunger, and undergoing fear, anger, and other passions. So my "picture" of its mind will not be empty, even though some details will be missing or appear spurious.

10. We may remember that the imagination we called objective is mediated by the data of such objective perceptions as sight and hearing. To imagine an elephant is to imagine seeing an elephant, and to imagine a thunderbolt is to imagine hearing a thunderbolt. This fact imposes an obvious restriction on the domain of things that can be thus imagined. As the practice of subjective imagination is confined to actions and states with experiential content, so the exercise of objective fantasy is restricted to the representation of objects with visual, auditory, and otherwise sensory aspects. For this reason one cannot imagine numbers, classes, human rights, or moral virtues. Thus not everything that exists, or is logically possible, is imaginable. Even the "pure" imagination, often invoked in geometry, is but an abstraction. You know that the straight line touches the circle at one point only in the plane, you know that the chiliagon has one thousand sides, you know that the hyperbola meets its asymptotes in infinity, and then you try to sharpen your mental vision by "zooming in", as it were, to reveal the finer and finer details . . . till you stop. And as you need no eyes to imagine, you need no microscopes to see the minutiae: whatever can be seen (heard, felt, etc.) can be imagined, but no more. As the limits of subjective experience are the limits of subjective fantasy, so the domain of objective imagination exhausts the world of possible experience.

It appears, then, that both the subjective and the objective creations of fantasy use the same material: imagined experiences. Both are constructions out of the elements of that material, but according to different principles of synthesis. In the subjective case the aim is to represent a consciousness, one's own, or someone else's, at a given point of life-history. In the objective case the purpose is to represent a thing as it appears in the field of experience. Notice, moreover, that in either case the rule of imaginary reconstruction is the idea one has about the thing to be represented in the one way or the other.

In the objective synthesis this idea is to be accounted for in terms of concept and schema. If, for instance, I want to imagine a tiger drinking out of a stream, it is not enough to have the concepts of a tiger (large Asiatic striped feline quadruped), of a stream, and of drinking.

I must also know what tigers, streams, and acts of drinking look like. And such knowledge cannot merely consist in the possession of a "static" image: something like a remembered snapshot. For I am able to imagine that scene in a great variety of detail and perspective: the tiger standing or crouching, seen frontally or sideways, and so forth. Thus I must have an active data-processing machinery at my disposal, which is capable of transforming the sensuous images of tigers, etc., which I have in my memory, into an inexhaustible array of presentations in which tigers may appear in my fancy. 'This schematism', rhapsodizes Kant ' . . . is an art concealed in the depths of the human soul, whose real modes of activity nature is hardly likely ever to allow us to discover.'[2] Kant may have been wrong about this forecast, but he was absolutely right about the necessity of schemata, both for our ability to imagine things, and also for all acts of recognition.

For it is the possession of a schema, and the affinity just mentioned between perception and imagination, which enables one to recognize, say, a tiger for what it is, as well as to recognize a particular face, or house, and the like. It is certainly not by virtue of any conceptual knowledge that I am able to recognize a person; nor would mere snapshot memory account for my recognizing him with an altered expression on his face, or from a new point of view. Actual perception must fit into the appropriate presentation of the perceived object, evoked in the imagination by the operation of the right schema, to become perception of *that* thing (my house), or of *such* thing (a tiger). For concepts alone, as Kant pointed out, have no affinity with perceptions.[3] This is not to deny, however, that one can acquire a schema by conceptual means, e.g. via verbal description of a certain kind of beast, or of an individual criminal. Schemata themselves may be the result of a synthesis.

Turning now to the subjective exercise of imagination, the first thing to notice is the fact that it has to follow the result of the objective exercise. In order to represent Napoleon's mind at the battle of Waterloo, for instance, one has to know enough about him, and about that battle, to be able to envisage the physical circumstances of his body on that occasion. For these conditions, together with the previous history of his life, provide the basis for the work of subjective imagination. Thus, in every case of transference the objective perception, real or imaginary, has to come first: one has to see, with the eyes of the

[2] *Critique of Pure Reason* A141, B180 (KS, 183).
[3] Ibid. A140–142, B179–181 (KS, 182–3).

body or of the mind, the circumstances of the person or the animal, to be able to imagine what it must be like for it to be in that situation.[4] Only, as we remember, whereas the bodily senses may suffice for the first task, imagination provides the only means for the second.

There is, moreover, a striking analogy between actual perception in the objective domain, and actual experience attributed to one's own subject. As my perception *of a tiger* becomes that by fitting into a "tiger presentation" produced by the appropriate schema in my imagination, so any real experience is perceived *as mine* inasmuch as it fits into the imaginary expectations produced by the "schema of subjectivity" applied to the known condition of my body. Thus the very same item of visual experience may be viewed as perception of a tiger (objective synthesis), and as my experience (subjective synthesis).

11. This is the time to discuss a problem often raised in connection with imagination, namely, whether there are such things as mental images: to put it more precisely, whether in imagining something objectively one has to create a representative entity, a mental picture, in which then that object is perceived. This idea might arise as follows. When I see a picture of the Escorial, for instance, there are two things on which I may focus my attention. First, there is the representative entity: that picture in front of me, a piece of printed paper in a frame. Second, the thing represented: that building, by no means made of paper, which I see in the picture. But when I actually see the Escorial, there is no picture involved: it is the building itself that I see, and not a building in a picture. But, the argument goes, when I imagine the Escorial, I do not have it in front of me; consequently in imagining the Escorial I must create a mental representation, make up a mental picture, to be able to see that building in it. The only difference seems to be that in the former case the picture is a physical object, made of paper or some other stuff, whereas in the latter case it is a mental entity, consisting of some more subtle material.

This problem is not likely to arise in connection with subjective fantasy. In imagining doing something, being in some state or another, or fancying being someone else, there is obviously no medium required besides the self: it is my consciousness that I modify in imagination to achieve these ends; I myself am the paper on which these "pictures" are drawn. For it is a subject I represent, a perceiver that is, and not something distinct from it to be perceived.

[4] This claim will be qualified in Chapter IV.

If this is so, then we have our first argument against the mental-image view. Above we succeeded in reducing the feats of objective fantasy to the exercise of subjective imagination. Now, if the latter endeavour does not require mental images, nor can the former, since it is of the same kind, albeit of a more restricted scope. Remember: to imagine an elephant is to imagine seeing an elephant. But seeing an elephant is a piece of visual experience which does not contain seeing any picture. And this is the experience I imagine having; the modality of imagination affects the experience, not its object. An imagined elephant is not a picture-elephant seen with real vision; it is a real elephant perceived in imagination.

Let us, consider, once more, the case of looking at a picture of the Escorial. Depending on my attention, I can see either of two things. I can see, first, the picture itself; after all, it is a physical object of certain dimensions, of certain material, which is located at some distance, at a given angle, in front of me. But then, second, I can see, if I so choose, the Escorial itself—not in a frame, but among the hills, at a distance and angle given by the perspective of the picture: close up, far away, sideways, or from above. And this perspective has nothing to do with how far away, or which way, I hold that picture in front of my face. There are, of course, many complexities affecting the notion of seeing something in a picture, but I leave those to the aestheticians. The rough description I gave is more than enough to our purpose.

As with any perception, seeing a picture of the Escorial can be imagined. In this case I have to visualize the picture itself: an object of a certain size and appearance, with distance, angles, and so forth, more or less determined. Then again, if I so choose, I can shift the focus of my fancy to see the Escorial in that picture. Just imagine being in the Rijksmuseum and looking at Rembrandt's *Nightwatch*; you can imagine the display of the picture: frame, lighting, and so on; or you can imagine seeing those people in the picture.

Now, the point is that there is no such duplicity in just imagining an elephant, the Escorial, the Battle of Waterloo, or what have you. There is but one perspective, not two. As in simple vision, there is no *medium in quo* consciously perceived, so in visualizing something one is not aware of a third entity between that thing and oneself.

The temptation to smuggle mental images into the exercise of imagination will further diminish as we consider non-visual fantasies: imagining the roar of canons, the smell of onions, the heat of the sun, or pain in one's molar. Where is the picture here?

Again, remember those "combined" exercises of real vision and imagination: trying to place a picture on the wall, or to envisage one's wife in the dress seen in the shop window. Does the "mental picture" contain the real things one sees?

We do, of course, talk of mental images harmlessly. After all, we speak of sights, images, or even pictures, in connection with real vision too. We visit the Escorial to do some sightseeing, and indeed, what an impressive picture it is, so suddenly rising among the lonely hills. And so we do have mental images, and do evoke mental pictures, if you please—but it is not an image, or a picture, that we fancy seeing in doing so.

These remarks are sufficient to disarm the trite objection made against the reality of sensory imagination, mentioning tigers and their stripes.

Suppose I tell you that I just imagined the tiger I had seen yesterday in the Zoo. 'How many stripes does the tiger you just imagined have', you ask. My answer might be this: 'Go there and count them.' For we are talking about a given real tiger, so I am entitled to interpret your question in a *de re* sense. But you insist: 'I do not mean that; I want to know with how many stripes did you imagine it.' Now, if my imagining of that tiger—or of an indefinite tiger for that matter—consisted in making up a mental picture of a tiger, then even this question would have an answer: as many stripes as that picture shows. But since what I imagined is the experience of seeing a tiger, it need not have. Experiences have no stripes, and the experience of seeing a tiger usually does not include counting its stripes. One can see, or imagine seeing, tigers or other striped stuff without counting, or even being able to count, the stripes. 'But in reality you could count if you went closer to the beast' you say. And so can I do in fantasy, I reply, if I focus my mental vision on the tip of its tail and start counting: one, two, three . . . After all, if I can count sheep in a sleepless night, why not stripes on a tiger's tail? But the operation of counting which I thus imagine doing is quite distinct from the mere perceiving of the tiger or the sheep. Accordingly I may have visualized a tiger without being able to tell how many stripes I saw.

But you are still unhappy about the idea of counting things in imagination: 'It is not really counting, because, for one thing, you cannot be mistaken, as you can in counting real things.' Sure enough, I reply, experiences are not like prisoners in the yard who stay around to be recounted or re-examined at will, so I cannot find out that I was wrong in labelling or counting them in the first place. This does not mean, however, that experiences cannot be recognized or counted as they occur. Suppose I have an injured tooth which gives me a stab of pain from time to time. Can I not count the stabs that occur during the time it takes to drink my soup? True, when I finish I may have the impression that I missed a stab or counted one too many. And so can I have the impression that I went wrong in counting sheep or stripes; but who can tell? Thus I realize that I could have been mistaken, yet am unable to correct the error. What would be the point of asking how many stars you are able to spot *now* in the Pleiades, if subjective things were not real and countable?

12. The contexts exemplified by (1) and (2) above do not exhaust the grammatical possibilities open to the verbs *imagine* and *fancy*. Consider the following occurrences:

> Can you imagine what would happen if Iran developed the H-bomb?
> Just imagine that there is life on Mars
> I can pretty well imagine why he did it

It is immediately obvious that these sentences do not reflect the "vicarious experience" of sensory imagination. To begin with, there is no way of inserting a perceptual verb after *imagine* in these examples. *Imagine there is life on Mars* does not mean *Imagine seeing* (or *hearing*, etc.) *that there is life on Mars*. Three consequences follow: first, *imagine* cannot be replaced by *picture* or *visualize*; second, the typically perspectival aspect of sensory imagination is missing; and third, the characteristic adverb, *vividly*, is out of place. What would it be like to picture the consequences of such a development in Iran from above; or to visualize why he killed the grocer vividly? It appears, therefore, that the verb *imagine* does not function here as an aspectual verb, but rather as a propositional verb on its own, semantically quite similar to *suppose*, *think of*, *guess*, etc. What these contexts call for is an exercise of reasoning: to think of certain possibilities, their consequences, implications, and the like.

There is nothing surprising in such an extended employment of *imagine*. It is well known that many straight perceptual verbs (particularly *see*, *hear*, and *feel*) have similar propositional uses. 'Now I see that you are right'; 'You lost your job, I hear'; 'He agreed, but I felt otherwise'; and so forth. Now, since the primary sense of *imagine* is often tied to the primary senses of these perceptual verbs, it is quite natural to see it follow them into the propositional domain. Consider the following exchange in which the propositional *see* matches the propositional *imagine*: 'Imagine what would happen if Iran had the H-bomb'; 'I can pretty well see what would happen . . . '

Human beings are not angels or animals. Our minds consist in an interplay of sensory and intellectual processes. As perception is captured in concepts and propositions, so thought, in its turn, is usually accompanied by the sensory flight of fancy. So one must not think that the double role of the verb *imagine* we have outlined corresponds to a neat duality of the mental operations it is used to designate. In visualizing the Battle of Waterloo one's mind goes on thinking about strategic matters, and in thinking about the reasons for the grocer's murder one is likely to picture him in his shop. Not to mention the fact that the exercise of the imagination is guided by our concepts and schemata and, if tied to reality, then it is by virtue of the provenance of some of these.

13. Imagination is not the only form of vicarious experience. Dreams and memory represent two other kinds, as we have mentioned in connection with time determination. I take this opportunity, therefore, to say a few words on memory, for this faculty will play a large role in a later part of this study.

The key verbs are *remember* and *recall*. These two are near-synonyms; accordingly, for the time being at least, I shall proceed on the assumption that what is sauce for the goose is sauce for the gander.

My basic claim is simple: these verbs may function as aspectual verbs in exactly the same way as *imagine* and *fancy* do. This use may be exhibited in the following sentences:

> I vividly recall walking on the Acropolis
> I still remember hearing Hitler on the radio
> Do you remember that truck bearing down on us?

The first is a typical "subjective" sentence; what I recall is my experience of walking on the Acropolis. The second is "objective", with the perceptual verb given: hearing Hitler on the radio, not seeing him on the balcony. The last lacks the perceptual verb, but not the perspective: what you might remember is seeing (and, perhaps, even hearing) the truck approaching rapidly towards us.

Thus far, then, there is no difference between the verbs of fantasy and the verbs of recollection. The first difference appears as we try to match the power of imagination in representing oneself objectively, with the resources of memory. Remember, there was no difficulty in imagining yourself in the water, while sitting on the cliff, and a fashion model can see herself, with the mind's eye, walking down the aisle, while walking down the aisle. There is no such performance possible for memory; even if I say, sloppily I think,

I remember myself walking down the Champs-Élysées

what I mean cannot be the objective performance. For one thing, seen from where do I remember myself? 'Seen from a large mirror in the shopwindow', you suggest, and you may be right. But this is, once more, a subjective situation, with unchanged perspective. No mirror is required, on the other hand, to *imagine* yourself walking down the Champs-Élysées, at this moment, and you can do it from any point of view you prefer.

The explanation of this difference is obvious yet important: one cannot remember seeing onself from a different perspective, simply because it is impossible *to have seen oneself* from an outside perspective. And by *oneself* I mean oneself, and not one's mirror image, photographic representation, or similar replica. This conclusion, of course, is nothing but a corollary to the truism that one cannot remember doing something that one has not done.[5]

14. Having done the thing is a necessary condition for the recollection of doing it, but by no means a sufficient one. There are many things I have done which, fortunately or unfortunately, I do not remember doing. I know, for I was told, that I broke a valuable plate at the age of three, but I do not recall doing it; I know, from the stamp on my passport, that I entered Bulgaria on 27th June 1967, but I do not remember crossing the border on that day, or any day. But since I now know what I did on these two occasions, tomorrow I may remember that I broke the plate or crossed the border. In other words, it is quite possible to remember (here *recall* fits less) having done something, or remember that one did something, without remembering (or recalling) doing that thing.

[5] One advantage of viewing *remember* and *recall* as aspectual modals is the ease with which we are able to explain troublesome sentences like

Only Churchill remembers giving the speech about blood, sweat, toil and tears

Indeed, why not? After all, I remember that Caesar crossed the Rubicon, that Kant died in 1804, that the square root of 169 is 13, and so forth. Yet, clearly, the fact that I remember that Caesar crossed the Rubicon does not entitle me to claim that I remember Caesar crossing the Rubicon. I indeed recall, quite vividly at that, Ruby shooting Oswald, but I cannot possibly recall, vividly or faintly, Brutus stabbing Caesar. I can do the first, because to recall Ruby shooting Oswald means to recall seeing Ruby shooting Oswald, and I did see, albeit on television, Ruby shooting Oswald. On the contrary, however, I cannot recall Brutus stabbing Caesar, simply because I did not see Brutus stabbing Caesar; thus I cannot recall seeing Brutus stabbing Caesar.

15. These considerations point to a distinction between an experiential use of *remember* and *recall*, and a propositional use of *remember*, and to a lesser extent *recall*, which is somewhat analogous to the distinction found in this respect in the uses of *imagine*.

As with *imagine*, the experiential use is either subjective or objective, the latter being nothing but a special case of the former, inasmuch as the object reproduced is mediated via the objective perception of sight and hearing. The difference, however, between fantasy and remembrance is the following: whereas the domain of imagination extends to all possible experience, the domain of memory is restricted to things experienced in the subject's actual past.

The propositional use of *remember*, on the other hand, is by no means confined to the subject's past history, but extends to all the facts he has learned in the past and did not forget. The element of past acquisition is essential. There are things that I just know at present without having learned them, in any reasonable sense, in the past. I know that I am alive, that I am wide awake, that I am sitting, that I am a man, and so forth, yet it does not make sense to say that I remember these things.

It is very interesting to notice that the verb *forget*, which is generally

(mentioned by Fodor in *The Language of Thought*, pp. 113 ff.), or

> Only Neil Armstrong remembers first stepping on the Moon, but many of us remember him doing it.

The analysis offered for (1) and (2) above explains the difference between what only they can recall, and what we can too. What Churchill and Armstrong can recall is their experience of doing those things; but what we recall is our experience of *hearing* Churchill (on the radio) or *seeing* Armstrong (on TV). In other words, the aspectual *remember* or *recall* is affixed to *giving a speech* or *stepping*, in their case; but to *seeing* or *hearing* in ours.

regarded as the opposite of *remember*, matches only the propositional sense of the latter verb. I may forget my name, what I ate for breakfast, who killed Oswald, and so forth. On the other hand, *forget* cannot replace *remember* and *recall* in experiential contexts. Let us try:

> I forgot walking on the Acropolis
> I forgot hearing Hitler on the radio
> I forgot the truck bearing down on us

These sentences are wrong, or, at best, are nothing but sloppy ways of saying that one forgot some fact once known, e.g. that I walked on the Acropolis, heard Hitler on the radio, etc. The point is, however, that *remember* and *recall* in similar contexts are by no means equivalent to the corresponding propositional versions. I vividly recall the bombing of Budapest in World War II. This fact is certainly not equivalent to the fact that I remember that Budapest was bombed in World War II. For one thing, you can remember the latter too, but not the former if you were not there at that time.

Even in a first person case, the two kinds of recollection are separable, thus distinct, with respect to the very same event. I have mentioned my crossing the Bulgarian border: I remember having done so, but I do not remember doing it. On the other hand, one may recall doing something without remembering that one did that thing. The teetotaller is given champagne in a ·pop-bottle, and, indeed, he takes it as soda-pop. He likes it, and remarks the next day: 'I still remember the taste of that stuff you gave me yesterday'. What does he recall? Well, the taste of champagne, and not the taste of soda-pop, to be sure; but he does not know it. Therefore, although he remembers the taste of champagne, he does not remember having had champagne. Experiential contexts are transparent, propositional ones opaque: seeing Mount Everest is seeing Chomolungma, recalling seeing Mount Everest is recalling seeing Chomolungma, but remembering that one has seen Mount Everest is not the same as remembering that one has seem Chomolungma. For one might now know that Mount Everest is Chomolungma.

IV

Traces of Individuals

1. IN CHAPTER II we postponed the discussion of the following problem. How is it possible for someone to form a representation of an individual, often remote in space and time, in spite of the fact that any such representation is bound to be incomplete and erroneous in many details? Suppose I am reading a history of the Punic Wars, and vividly imagine Hannibal on the battlefield of Cannae. I seem him there, among his aides, giving orders and surveying the scene; I even try to imagine what it must have been like to view the carnage with his one eye, with feelings of triumph and pity mingling in his heart. Now, do I know exactly what he looked like, where he stood (on horseback or on foot), what he really felt, and so forth? Surely not. Then what makes me think that it is *he* whom I just evoked in my fancy? For it certainly would be false and stultifying to say that no one can imagine a historical person, or a scene of history, short of complete accuracy of representation. It is taken for granted that we all do these things, and some of us (think of Robert Graves writing *I Claudius*) are masters of this art. What is then the link that connects the defective images in our minds to their originals?

At the time of our first mentioning of this matter, we reflected on the analogous situation of painting a picture of a historical figure, or of a past event. Do the millions of pictures of Christ represent him accurately—from the images of a serene Roman nobleman found in the catacombs, to the melancholy ascetic of the 15th century? And we know that Leonardo was all wrong in the details of the *Last Supper* (they did not *sit* at meals) . . .

'So what,' you say, 'what does it matter? After all, those painters meant to depict Christ, or the Last Supper, and from internal and external evidence we are able to gather their intention.' Of course this is the answer; but what does it mean? What does it mean to say that Leonardo, for instance, intended to paint Christ and the Apostles when he set out in that refectory in Milan? 'Well, he had Christ in mind, to begin with . . . ' How true, I reply, but this answer just pushes the problem back where it was before: how could Leonardo, or we for that matter, have Christ "in mind"? Is it because we possess a complete and accurate image of him in our thoughts, or at least one which is "more true" of him than of anybody else? If the former alternative were the case most problems of theology could be solved in no time. About the latter, just ask yourself how much of a little old lady's image of Christ must actually fit him to be that, the image of Christ . . .

2. Fortunately for us, a recent development in the theory of reference offers hope of breaking out of this circle. I think of the "causal", "genetic", or "historical" account developed by Kaplan, Kripke, Donnellan, and others. In Kripke's version, for instance, it is the causal link connecting the name of an individual to the individual itself, rather than the "fitting" or accuracy of the accompanying descriptions, that enables a speaker to refer to that individual by the use of the name.[1] But we are not so much interested in names, descriptions, and reference; our primary concern is not with speech-acts, but with thought. Moreover, since speech is but the expression of thought, the root of the problem must lie there: what we obviously need is a causal or historical account of mental representations of individuals. Kaplan's paper "Quantifying In" indeed contains the seeds of the needed theory, and the following explanation is but a development of his views.[2] As he puts it, a subject "knows" an individual if he is in possession of a "vivid name" *of* that individual. The vividness corresponds to the subjective "descriptive content" of the mental representation (roughly, one's "core-beliefs" about the individual), whereas the particle *of* requires a genetic account causally linking the acquisition of that representation to the individual itself. Thus a child may have a rich, vivid "name" of Santa Claus without its being *of* anything. On the contrary, my notion of Kalgoorlie, Australia, is not very vivid, yet is *of* Kalgoorlie (via the natives, the settlers, the surveyors, maps, atlases, and my looking at atlases).

The "vivid name," i.e. the subject's mental image of the individual in question, is likely to be a heterogeneous bundle: besides conceptual elements (that is, the propositions one believes about that individual) it may contain sensory parts: a miscellany of remembered or evoked shapes, colours, and other impressions, to be integrated into a "schema"

---

[1] In *Naming and Necessity*.
[2] In the sequel I shall use some of Kaplan's phrases in his sense: e.g. (*vivid*) *name*, being *en rapport* with something, *leaving a mark* on somebody.

to facilitate imaginary reproduction. For that matter, even proper names, such as *Kalgoorlie*, are sensory patterns of sound and shape. Some of these elements may be false, wrong, or distorted, without harm to identification if the causal pedigree of the whole remains intact.

The causal account, admittedly, is but a cover-story, suggestive and attractive in spite of, perhaps even because of, its vagueness. There are many ways in which a representation can be "caused" in the human mind. This is the time to go into some details and flesh out the story. In doing so I shall go beyond the domain of mental representations, and add some remarks on reference and verbal introduction, not only because of the interconnectedness of these concepts, but also because of the role these last two notions are going to play in a later part of this work.

3. Think of a writer, composing a novel in his head. In doing so he may compile a very vivid "name", i.e. a coherent and detailed idea of a person, beast or town, equipped with proper names, places and times, without, in doing so, thinking *of* anything. But when he thinks of his editor he *knows* he is playing another game. How does he? The answer is as simple as obvious: he *remembers* the editor, but not his hero. But, you object, tomorrow he may remember the hero he fancied up today, too. True, I answer, he may remember what his hero is *like*, as he remembers what his editor is like; but, in addition, he will also *recall meeting* the editor, *reading* his letters, which he cannot do in regard to his hero. He will know, in other words, that his representation of the editor is derived from his perception of the editor (or some such tokens related to him as those letters) preserved in his memory.

The police, in order to facilitate the apprehension of the culprit, often asks the victim of crime to describe, or even to draw, the criminal "from memory". He is instructed to recall, as vividly as he can, the man, his voice, and his deeds. And, as a result of this effort, he may come up with more and more details, adding up to a fairly complete description. The "vivid name" thus compiled, and transmitted to the police, is derived from his memory of that experience. I want to distinguish, therefore, on the basis of what we found in the previous chapter, the memory of experience, i.e. the kind of memory only the victim can have of the criminal, from the memory of propositions, i.e. the kind of memory of the criminal which the police too can share. The grammatical forms of the sentences used in speaking about these two kinds of recollection are indicative, albeit not decisive by themselves. Compare the following two statements:

(1) I remember that Brutus stabbed Caesar
(2) I recall Ruby shooting Oswald

The first statement means that I have learned that fact and have not yet forgotten. The second means that I recall *seeing* (or otherwise perceiving) that event. The permissible adverbs point in the same direction. (1) admits things like *from school*, or *from reading Suetonius*; (2) takes *vividly, on TV*, and not the other way around. Obviously, then, the form of (2) is not suitable for things I could not have experienced, because I was not there (not even via TV), or was not even alive. Only Neil Armstrong can recall stepping first on the moon, and only those who watched him can recall him taking that first step, but we all remember that he did.

Then compare these statements:

(3) I remember that I crossed the Bulgarian border in June, 1967
(4) I remember (recall) crossing the Bulgarian border in June, 1967

(3), as we may recall from Chapter III, may be true in the following situation: yesterday I looked into my old passport and found the appropriate stamp. So I learned the fact, and today I still remember it. This, however, by no means guarantees the truth of (4): I may have no recollection of crossing that border at all; I do not even "faintly" (notice the adverb) remember doing so.

But then suppose that both (3) and (4) are true, and I vividly recall the harrowing experience of crossing that border. One day my wife remarks: 'Remember all that hassle we had at the Turkish border in '66'. Now I know that she is just mistaken; what she remembers is crossing the Bulgarian border in '67. Yet, obviously she does not remember *that* we crossed that border in '67. Thus statements such as

A remembers V-ing . . .
A remembers that he V-ed . . .

do not entail each other.

This fact is connected with another difference we brought out in the previous chapter. Seeing Mount Everest is seeing Chomolungma, and recalling seeing Mount Everest is recalling seeing Chomolungma. Remembering, on the other hand, *that* one has seen Mount Everest is not the same as remembering *that* one has seen Chomolungma. For one might not know that Mount Everest is Chomolungma. Contexts of experience, and of experiential memory, are transparent, but contexts of propositional memory are opaque. The reason is that in the second case there is a subjective representation, a "name" involved, but not in the first. Sensation (and the memory of sensation) has no conscious medium, no *signum in quo*; it is not a representation of the object which is consciously perceived or remembered, but the object itself.

This distinction can be expressed in the following way, too. Those who watched the dismal scene in Dallas not only remember who Ruby was, but also remember Ruby. Those who did not may remember the first thing, but not the second. Similarly, although most of us know who Brutus was, no one alive can remember Brutus. In such contexts the phrase *who Ruby was*, stands for some facts about Ruby, but the name *Ruby, tout court*, stands for Ruby himself.

Thus, the person who watched Ruby kill Oswald on TV remains *en rapport* with Ruby, not only because he possessed a notion *of* Ruby, e.g. 'the short fat man who killed Oswald' (he may not know his name, and this "description" need not be verbalized), but also because he remembers the man himself. Thus he is aware not only of the representation, but of its link to its original. The second element, the memory of experience, may fade away with time, yet the first, the representation, may remain. In seeing a picture, encountering a name, or reading a description, we often ask 'Where did I see that man?', in trying to revive the source of that representation. This, incidentally, is the point of displaying "Wanted" notices at the post-office, adorned with appropriate mug-shots and descriptions.

Thus, we see that the first and most immediate way of getting acquainted with an individual is via sense perception. In this case the subsequent representation is derived from the very perception, or the memory thereof, of the individual itself. I shall call this, quite naturally, "firsthand" acquaintance.

4. There are, however, an immense number of other individuals who are known to us (of whom we can think, and to whom we can refer), yet we have never encountered them in the flesh. Brutus and Caesar are just two of them. We do not remember Caesar in the way we remember Oswald, but we know *of* him: have heard and read of him, looked at his pictures in books and his busts in museums. By these means he has been introduced to us—"second-hand", as it were.

What lies in the background of such an introduction? Well, the existence of an unbroken causal chain leading, for example, from Caesar to my idea of him. On the far end, there is Caesar and the people perceiving him. These people, who are thus acquainted with him "first hand", form representations of him, and some of these, then, are transmitted, in speech, writing, and images, from generation to generation, till they reach us and make up our image of Caesar. Causal stories of this kind have been discussed, very suggestively albeit sketchily, in recent literature. So I do not have to go into the various vicissitudes these representations might undergo along their historical path, such as distortion, fusion, splitting, blockage, and so forth; nor into such correcting measures as statements of identity, of non-existence, and the like. What we have added to the story, however, is a more complete explanation of the beginning of the causal chain: how experience gets converted, as it were, into a representation. Later on, in discussing the linguistic details of "second-hand" introductions, we shall obtain a clearer perception of the nature of the links that make up the chain.

It appears, then, that a person may have second-hand acquaintance with an individual without knowing that he does. This, as we recall, is usually not the case with firsthand acquaintances. There, the "name" is connected to the memory of experience in the subject's mind. This is missing in second-hand acquaintances. True, the subject may recall *learning* about the individual, but this is a poor substitute. For think of the following case. Grandfather tells stories to Johnny at bedtime. One night he tells the story of Hercules, the next night the story of Hannibal. Johnny is thus "acquainted" with Hercules, and acquainted with Hannibal. He may take both persons for real or neither, it does not matter; Hannibal "left a mark on him" anyway, but not Hercules. The causal chain of representations leads to a real man in the one case, but is "blocked" in the other.[3] Again, think of the disappointment of the pious who were told a few years ago by the Pope that their favourite saint, Christopher, George, or Barbara, did not exist.

At any rate, well-connected representations, firsthand or secondhand, are "rigid designators" in Kripke's sense,[4] not by virtue of their descriptive content, but because of the historical tie to their sources. A picture *of* Caesar, even a bad picture of Caesar, could not be *of* anybody else.

And this is not a matter of proper names. As we are going to see,

[3] In Donnellan's sense. See his 'Speaking of Nothing'.
[4] See his *Naming and Necessity*.

such names are very important for the purposes of reference, but they are not indispensable, and a representation may be rigidly designating even without a name. Think of a young man who literally "lost his shirt" in the scuffle following Christ's arrest.[5] We don't know his name or anything else about him, and probably never will. Yet, if the gospels are true, he is firmly established in history, woven into its texture by the thread of that single description. Once more, it is not the descriptive content that achieves identification, but the force of testimony by a witness (presumably St. Mark) based on the memory of his experience. For, as far as the content goes, that description could be true even if some other young man had suffered that misfortune instead of the one who actually did. On the contrary, St. Mark's report would retain its identifying force even if it were, in part, erroneous. For it was dark, so it may have been a cotton and not linen piece the lad had on, and perhaps the "young man" was really a girl. In any case, St. Mark had him (her) in mind in writing the story, and so do we, once we have read it.

5. We have just implied that the causal antecedents of a picture, or representation, belong to the "essence" of that picture. Caesar's name, description, or bust can designate rigidly only if its nexus to Caesar is a necessary one. This accords with the intuition, nicely brought out by Kripke, that "insertion into history" belongs to the essence of individuals in a very broad sense (including things like rivers, nations, and regiments). So why not of representations, in an equally broad sense?

The idea of the rigidity of the causal nexus leads us to the last, and weakest, way of introduction: acquaintance not first or second-hand, but really no hand at all.

Robinson Crusoe finds that footprint on the beach. Is he then, already, acquainted with its maker? Yes, if *that* footprint could not have been made by anybody but that person. And, if I am right, then it could not have. *Ergo*, he is.

Then think of the painter known as the Master of the Aix Annunciation. His real name is unknown, and, maybe, we don't know anything else about him either. Even so, since nobody but he could have painted that picture, he is part of history, hanging there, as it were, on a single thread.

[5] 'And there followed him a certain young man, having a linen cloth cast about his naked body; and the young men laid hold on him: and he left the linen cloth and fled from them naked' (Mark 15: 51-2.)

This situation reminds us of Donnellan's famous 'Smith's murderer' in the first instance, i.e. when the body foully done in has just been discovered.[6] Donnellan claims that if the identity of the murderer is not yet known, then the description is used attributively. Since we are not talking yet about uses of descriptions, but rather of representations entertained in thought, I shall say that I agree with him to the following extent: the content of that description, that concept, if you like, certainly can be thought of attributively, as all representations can. For all of them can be viewed in abstraction from the causal link, if there is one, tying them to an individual; that nexus is not part of the representation. Just as the fact that a painting is *of*, say, Charles the Fifth, is not part of that painting. Thus, one can think of the Master of the Aix Annunciation attributively: what kind of painter, what kind of man, he *must* have been . . . (notice the modality). Similarly, Robinson (and *a fortiori* Sherlock Holmes if he had been there) could have concluded many things about the person, *whoever he was*, who left that footprint behind.

What I do not accept is the suggestion that Smith's murderer (and the Master of the Aix Annunciation, etc.) is not known. In a sense he is known, if he killed Smith, by that very act. For no one else but he could have done *that* deed. True, his *identity* is unknown. But this merely means that we have no *other* link to him. So we cannot say: 'The murderer of Smith = A' as we can say 'The murderer of Oswald = Ruby'. For Ruby is known to us (via the Dallas police, CIA) even apart from that murder. So, when the police set out to apprehend Smith's murderer, they are not trying to capture an individual answering a certain description (this may be the beginning of the investigation), but the one who actually *did* the murder. And, if they hope for conviction, they had better find *witnesses who saw* him do it (or leave the scene). For if not, their case will be "circumstantial", i.e. having a man who *could* be the murderer (fits the descriptions available), but again might not be. Descriptions do not identify, witnesses do.[7]

Are we not acquainted, in a very real sense, with the otherwise unknown slave who left his footprint in King Tut's tomb? Or with the scribe who carved *that* particular hieroglyph into *that* stone four thousand years ago? Only Rembrandt could have painted *Nightwatch*, on two distinct accounts: first, speaking "attributively", nobody else

---

[6] In 'Reference and Definite Descriptions'.

[7] And things like fingerprint patterns, of course. But this is due to some contingent facts about human anatomy.

had the ability; and second, speaking "referentially", being painted by Rembrandt belongs to the essence of that painting. Perhaps this is the reason why a damaged Rembrandt is of far greater worth than a perfect copy of a perfect Rembrandt.

6. There are some notions, and corresponding descriptions, with the feature of uniqueness built into them on conceptual grounds. Thus they can be true of only one individual. Think of the idea of the tallest man who ever lived (and ignore the possibility of dead heat), and the like.

Such representations, clearly, are not rigid designators on their own, since, if you like to put it that way, they pick out different individuals in different possible worlds. Take two Roman gladiators, both extremely tall, whom we know of: Maximus and Longinus. It may be true that, if Maximus had been fed growth-hormones in his youth, then he would have become the tallest man, if Longinus, then he. But now assume that Longinus, *de facto*, was the tallest, but we don't know this. Can we, still, by a sheer effort of will, think of him (and refer to him), in terms of that notion, which, mind you, is not anchored in history? Kaplan recently came to think that we can.[8] With the intention of *Dthat* [*the tallest man* . . .], he implies, we can keep *him* constant in all possible worlds in which he exists, even if, in some of them, he is not the tallest (he dies in childhood).

I do not think that good intentions are enough in this matter, but intuitions may differ; here we are scraping the barrel of common sense. My reasons against Kaplan's recent view are the following.

First of all, in this case, contrary to all others, the representation *cannot* be, in part, wrong or mistaken. St. Mark's youth may have been wrapped in burlap (and, perhaps, it was a girl . . .), but the tallest man must be a man, and the tallest (at least in this world). The difference is the following: St. Mark has had "somebody in mind" whom he tried to describe (from memory), and could have gone wrong in doing so. But whom do I have in mind in thinking of the tallest man? Surely nobody in *that* sense. To put it roughly: I have a concept in mind, and not a man.

Suppose I write a letter to the Editor of the *Canberra Times* in which I claim that Mr. S. Zywczak (I picked the last entry from the telephone directory) is a spy. He has the right to sue me for libel. If, however, I write to the effect that the strongest man in Canberra is an extortionist, Mr. Kowalsky, who is the strongest, and knows it, has

[8] In 'Dthat'.

no grounds to sue, unless he knows that I know it too. If I can demonstrate that I do not, I may be guilty of a prank, but not of slander, since I do not have him (Kowalsky) in mind.

My friend, Orlando, comes to town, and, as usual, wants to meet the prettiest girl. I know that Esmeralda is the one. Is it true, then, that Orlando has Esmeralda in mind, that he wants to meet her? Compare this situation with the following. Orlando arrives with a copy of the local paper, with pictures of the charity ball. 'I want to meet that girl' he says pointing at an unnamed picture of Esmeralda. In this case there is no doubt: he wants to meet Esmeralda. 'I often thought of you since I saw that picture,' he avers truthfully when finally introduced. But what could he say in the first case? 'I often thought of you since I conceived the idea of the prettiest girl in town'? This might flatter Esmeralda, but flattery is no truth.

Moral: *S. Zywczak* in the directory is "taken from" S. Zywczak; that picture is "taken of" Esmeralda; but the notions of the strongest man and the prettiest girl are not taken from anybody. Therefore they do not suffice to represent those persons uniquely.

7. As a result of these considerations we now have an adequate idea of "having somebody (or something) in mind". On this basis the imagination can then proceed to represent that individual, following a schema which incorporates the applicable elements of its "vivid name". Of course, if one is interested in greater accuracy, one has to try to expand the base of the imaginary reproduction. In trying to evoke, for example, Napoleon's appearance at the battle of Waterloo in a realistic matter, one has to read up his life and the history of that battle, one has to visit the museums to contemplate his pictures and the garments of the day, and so forth. Yet none of these things are strictly necessary: the imagination can take off on the scantiest of grounds, and yet not lose the subject to be represented. We can, without the threat of absurdity or confusion, try to imagine the arrival of the runner of Marathon, or even the appearance of the prehistoric woman who left her footprint in the cave of Pech Merle.

Moreover, according to what we said in the previous chapters, once the "objective" representation is completed, it becomes possible to reproduce, by means of transference, the inner states of the characters thus evoked: of Napoleon, of Wellington, or even of that woman in the cave. Do we not try hard to imagine what the wall-painters of Lascaux must have felt and thought, and how they looked at the world?

In all these matters it is too much to hope for accuracy. But, I ask again, who can ever hope to paint a "faithful" image of Christ? Or of the early saints? I am quite sure that Dürer's *St. Jerome* bears no similarity to the Dalmatian . . . Then what is the point of producing these works under those labels? Well—idle curiosity aside—who really cares what, say, St. Jerome actually looked like? What matters is what kind of man he was. And the painter, by his artistic means, tries to express that; or at least he reveals how *he* sees his subject. Moreover, "the kind of man he was" is primarily an internal matter: character, thoughts, feelings, and the like. Dürer, Rembrandt, and other great artists, aim at drawing a soul as reflected in a face, bearing, and gesture.

In the previous chapters we remarked that the representation of another mind follows the imaginary reproduction of the body and its circumstances. But this move—at least in the works of an artist—may be reversed. The mind of Christ can be gathered from the gospels, and that of St. Jerome from his writings. Now the artist, and we too for that matter, try to create outward appearances to fit these minds— they on canvas, we in fancy. And in that sense, Rembrandt's Christ is a faithful representation—whether or not it conforms to the actual appearance of the historical Christ.[9]

8. 'You speak of a historical Christ', someone might say, 'and indeed, by virtue of the causal nexus you outlined you can speak *of* him. But what if—as some daring souls maintain—there was no historical Christ? What do you speak *of*, then, and whom do you reproduce on canvas or in your mind?'

In order to answer this question let us recall the examples of Hercules, Sherlock Holmes, and other worthies, "of" whom we have a vivid image, in spite of the fact that they did not exist in the real world. Using Donnellan's phrase, we said that in such cases the series of representations going back in time is "blocked" at a certain point. What does this mean? Simply the following: the origin of such a representation is "irregular", i.e. it does not first arise as a result of actual observations of an individual, preserved in memory, and converted into a "name" to be transmitted to others. The ultimate source of our image of Caesar is the perception of Caesar by his contemporaries. But there was no one who could have observed Hercules or Sherlock Holmes. True, as we admitted discussing "no hand" introductions, one can form an

---

[9] In this connection, too, think of pictures of angels, devils, or God the Father in Michelangelo's *The Creation of Adam*.

image of an individual by merely viewing one of his "works" (a painting, or a mere footprint). But, again, there are no such "works" attributable to Hercules or Holmes. Hercules's works, astonishing as they were, could no more be witnessed by real people then the hero himself.

The important thing to notice, however, is this. The trouble with, say, Hercules's image is not in the image, but in its origin. Hence, once such an image is given, it "behaves" in exactly the same way as images of real things behave. They are transmitted, acquired, and eventually distorted or altered in the same manner. Thus, even if one thinks that Hercules did but nine works, or that Holmes lived in Regent Street, one is mistaken about Hercules or Holmes. Once more, it is the causal link of acquisition, and not the accuracy of content, that determines the identity of the represented individual. 'But there is no individual', you object, 'thus one cannot even speak of correctness or accuracy in these cases.' This is false, of course: I just gave some examples of false beliefs about Hercules and Holmes. And, as any teacher can testify, students are often "factually" wrong about Achilles, Hamlet, or Lolita.

Yet the objector surely deserves an answer not a brush-off. In order to provide one, let us recall Aristotle's curious remarks about the "misfortunes" that can befall a deceased person: loss of fame, dishonour, and the like.[10] To some extent, at least, we all can say with the poet 'non omnis moriar'. Not only our "works" remain, but our "name", i.e. the traces we leave behind in the memory of posterity: the tail of the comet. Now, with real individuals the "comet" is complete: it consists of both nucleus and tail. Mythical, fictional, and other "nonexisting" beings are incomplete: they consist of a tail without a nucleus—to make a bad pun, they are instances of the tale wagging the dog.

Thus, as Caesar keeps existing in tradition, statues, books, and people's memory, so do Hercules and Sherlock Holmes. In Chapter II we claimed, following Kripke's doctrine, that the "essence" of an individual consists in its insertion into history: birth, origin, manufacture, and the like. *Mutatis mutandis*, the same is true of non-existing individuals: the 'essence" of Sherlock Holmes is tied to the creative work of Conan Doyle.[11] But, whereas in Caesar's case an

---

[10] *Eth. Nic.* I, 10. Did De-stalinization affect Stalin? Yes, he ceased to be the Teacher of Nations. Or, to mention a favourable development, one might say things like 'Kant influences an increasing number of philosophers these days.'

[11] Reflect on the expression: 'Holmes is Doyle's brainchild'.

actual individual is inserted into history to live on in real life and beyond in his "name", in Holmes's case it is the "name" itself which is inserted and left behind to follow its shadowy course of life.

Holmes's case is an easy one in this respect, since his origin is due to one writer (although, notice, some later authors tried to add to the legend . . .). Hercules, unfortunately, has a much more confused ancestry. Such looseness, however, need not worry us. Even with natural individuals the clarity of insertion ranges from that of a human to, say, that of a river. When, exactly, did the Mississippi originate?

Turning now to the matter of accuracy, my representation of Caesar may or may not conform to the prevailing opinion on Caesar. And this opinion, in turn, may be more or less true of the actual Caesar. With Sherlock Holmes and his ilk the fitting process has to end where (going back in time) the "name" ends, i.e. in Doyle's manuscripts, and similar sources.

Since, finally, the basis of my imaginary exercises is the "name" of the individual I intend to represent, and since Holmes's "name" is as good a "name" as Caesar's, I can represent either of them at will. I will know of course, that one of them did exist, the other did not. But thinking of Homer or Moses, I may be unsure, or may be mistaken, about existence. For I may be in exactly the same psychological state, whether or not the object of my fancy is a real person. Botticelli's Venus looks as real as one of his Madonnas. Both represent a definite individual; but only one of them did exist in reality. Compare this with such allegorical pictures as Dürer's *Melancholy*. It represents *a* woman, but it does not conform to any "name" of an individual, real or fictional, found in tradition. After all, we too can imagine *a* woman or *a* tiger, not just *the* woman we met last night, *the* heroine of the novel we are reading, or *the* tiger seen in the circus.

To conclude: I can imagine Sherlock Holmes, and I can imagine being Sherlock Holmes. For we represent him as a person and not as a robot. In doing so I conform to a pre-existing representation of an individual. That individual, incidentally, may be one's own creation: Doyle himself may have thought of Sherlock Holmes—after he has first conceived him in his mind.

But Holmes did not exist: i.e. his pre-existing representation does not belong to the "schema of reality".[12] In other words, the presentations his particular schema generates are not to be found in experience.

[12] See footnote 13, Chapter I.

But it remains the schema of a human individual: *the* one conceived by Conan Doyle as Sherlock Holmes.[13]

9. The idea of having a person or some other particular in mind provides the background for a theory of reference within the framework of a Gricean[13] view of communication.

The purpose of the act of referring to an individual is to evoke the thought of the same individual in the listener's mind. Hence the following seem to be the necessary conditions for a speaker A to refer to S in talking to B.

- (a) S must be known to A in the sense just explained.
- (b) A must assume that S is also known to B.
- (c) A must intend to say something about S.
- (d) A must find a "device of communication" such that, in his estimate, its perception will lead B to the thought of S as the individual A is talking about.

If all these conditions are fulfilled, then A can go on to the "execution" of reference, and if that is done properly (think of requirements of grammar, articulation, volume, etc.), then his reference to S will be "happy" in Austin's sense. Of course, not even a happy reference guarantees uptake. This feature is not peculiar to reference. There are many ways of being not understood or misunderstood.

10. Thus there is no possibility of reference without previous acquaintance, actual in the speaker, and presupposed in the addressee. To see this, think of the following extreme situation. An intelligent being, somehow endowed with the knowledge of English (which, mind you, does not contain proper names),[14] is translated to Earth from extragalactic space, and I meet him on an open field. My claim is this: in talking to him I could not refer to any individual except him and me and the ostensible features of that environment, simply because we would not have any common acquaintances beyond these. Nor could he, in talking to me, refer to anything else either.

Is there a way of extending the circle of our mutual acquaintances?

---

[13] I do not claim to have provided an "ontology" of non-existing beings. All I could do was to give an explanation of our ability to represent such entities.

[14] And ignore Putnam's remarks on natural kind words in his 'The Meaning of "Meaning" '.

Yes there is, as there is in polite society: by introducing my acquaintances to him, and the other way round. There is no reference without
previous acquaintance, and there is no acquaintance without introduction. Nothing prevents me, however, from doing the introducing
myself.

Such a need may arise even in the ostensive situation. There are
many things in one's field of vision which lie there unnoticed. One
might come to notice them, however, either spontaneously, or guided
by others. 'Let us sit down under that tree' I say to our cosmic guest,
accompanied by a suitable gesture of pointing. In this case, if he has not
noticed the tree before, introduction and reference go hand in hand,
jointly achieved by the same act of ostension.

This situation, however, is the exception rather than the rule. Introduction and reference are two distinct functions, and, normally, the
means of achieving them are equally distinct. This is a crucial, yet
perhaps the most neglected, aspect in the theory of reference.

11. In standard cases, of course, when not talking to "remote" beings
but to our neighbours, friends, and people sharing the same culture and
history, we do have a wide circle of common acquaintances. In talking
about them, no introduction is needed and the function of reference
operates alone. How does it?

Two persons have a common acquaintance if, and only if, each has
a representation (Kaplan's "name") of that individual. But, of course,
these representations are likely to differ in content. Nevertheless, in
most cases, there will be some common elements. It is by virtue of
these overlapping features, then, that the task of reference becomes
possible. If there are no common features, or if these are not "strong"
enough, then the task of reference has no hope of success.

I shall explain what I mean here, in an abstract fashion first. Suppose
A's representation of S consists of the elements a, b, c, d; and B's representation of S consists of the elements c, d, e, f. Then A, in referring
to S, has to rely on c and d to bring S to B's mind. That is to say, he
has to encode a subset of these features in the referring part of his
speech-act. But the question remains, whether the overlap, or the
chosen subset, is sufficient for B to "recognize" S by these means.
If, for example, the same elements, c, d, also figure in his idea of other
individuals, then, *per se*, it is not. Actual circumstances may improve
matters to some extent by "narrowing the scope" of B's search. In
talking about philosophy, for instance, the name *Aristotle* will lead the

hearer's mind to the Stagirite rather than to Onassis. Similarly, the phrase *that man* may suffice if, say, that man just finished his speech. There is no need to say more on this point, since daily life provides us with thousands of examples.

There is, however, a complicating factor. Speaking in terms of the general case we just discussed, the mere existence of an overlap between A's and B's representations of S is not sufficient for A to be able to refer to S; he must also know, or guess, that there is such an overlap, and what it contains. In other words, A must know, or guess, *how* if at all, S is represented to B.

The diplomat who tells us that he met Stalin in the thirties will not refer to him as the first Secretary of the Communist Party of the USSR; on the contrary, in telling us that he has met the Prime Minister of Botswana he is not likely to use his name alone. On the other hand, even a sloppy or inaccurate description will do if the speaker is sure that in the given circumstances its use will lead the hearer to the thought of the desired individual. Donnellan's 'Smith's murderer', in the second instance, is a case in point. The man sits there, accused of murder. Since both the speaker and the addressee are in the court-room, that phrase will suffice, whether or not that man is in fact the murderer.

We have noted above, in connection with Hannibal and Johnny, that one can have a well-connected representation of an individual without knowing that one has. And we argued, in general, that the provenance, or pedigree, of a representation is distinct from the representation itself. But now we are speaking of the act of reference, and, as we just discovered, the happy performance of this act is not possible if the speaker has no idea of, first, *whether* the individual he has in mind to speak about is represented to the addressee and, second, *how* it is represented. Since he cannot peer into his listener's mind, he has to make a guess concerning the ways in which that individual must have been, or is likely to have been, introduced to the listener. He must form a hypothesis, in other words, about the likely causal path producing a representation in the hearer's mind. But to do so, he must be clear about the ontological and historical status of the individual to be referred to: is it a historical character, mythical figure, literary creation, or what? And, in each case, how is it placed, what is its context? For without knowing these things he could not even begin to speculate about the likelihood and manner of its being represented to the addressee.

This "status" I am talking about, moreover, is a feature of the pedigree and not of the representation itself. Hamlet's ghost is a ghost, but Hamlet is a man. And Botticelli's *Venus* represents a woman, not a spirit. Again, a mythical beast is not a kind of beast in the sense that a marsupial is. The relevant difference between, say, our image of Caesar and our image of Hercules lies outside the image; it is the function of their origin: connected in the one case, and blocked in the other. But then, to be able to guess how, if at all, an individual is represented to you, I must have some information, and recollection, of how its idea has come down to me and might have reached you. Have I encountered it in life? When and where? Have I heard about it? By whom and in what context? Have I read about it? In what kind of source? Newspaper, history, fiction, or what?

Johnny remembers Hannibal only from his grandfather's bedtime stories. Jimmy, however, remembers reading about him in a history book. Thus Jimmy, but not Johnny, can confidently refer to him, by name or description (say, 'the general who led the elephants across the Alps'), in speaking to his history teacher. For he, the teacher, must have heard about him too.

The point holds regardless of the open or blocked source of the representation. I can confidently talk of King Kong and King Tut, but not of King Lear, to Los Angeles children; and of Deep Throat to truckdrivers and Watergate fans with different but predictable results. But to do this I must remember how I came to know these personages, for otherwise I would have no idea of how, if at all, they may be known to my audience.

And this is so, *a fortiori*, with respect to our closer and more private acquaintances: one's family, friends, colleagues, associates, and so forth. My words 'the girl who arrived late last night' will suffice to refer to her in talking to someone whom I remember from the party last night. 'The dog' will pick out Hector in the conversations of a family endowed with Hector, their only dog. For the speaker knows—not only Hector, but what they know . . .

12. Still, the most important referring devices are proper names. This is so simply because they are invented precisely to overcome the interpersonal divergence of individual representations, and the ensuing guesswork about common elements. Hegel is Hegel, never mind the very different beliefs you and I may hold about him. Provided, of course, that the pedigree of the name is authentic.

The idea of a proper name arises out of the realization that it is the causal link, and not the content, of a representation that achieves uniqueness. So even if the descriptive content is reduced to a minimum, (or, ideally, to zero), the representation still can serve, when expressed, to achieve reference. So names are introduced to neutralize the idiosyncratic differences in our representations of the same individuals. A name, to use our previous term, is an overlap by design.

But names, too, have to be introduced, their reference "fixed" by descriptive devices. From then on, however, the burden of rigid designation shifts to the name, and the descriptions become loose. 'Hannibal was the general who crossed the Alps with elephants, etc.' But, of course, he might have stayed in Spain, and never crossed the Alps. To express this we feel more at ease with the form 'Hannibal might not have crossed the Alps' than with the form 'The general who crossed the Alps . . . might not have crossed the Alps'. Both statements are true, but in the first the referring function is carried out by a "pure" device, untainted by descriptive elements, which come into conflict with the predicate in the second. Not to speak of the possibility of historians discovering that *Hannibal*, after all, did not cross the Alps but went around them. In the latter case we have to give up that part of the introductory description; but enough remains to give "sense" to the name. For some "sense" has to remain: the name has to "ring a bell" in people's minds; otherwise it is but empty sound. Think of *Aristotle*, the Stagirite to you, Ari to Jackie, and nothing to the illiterate. Names do not "stand for" descriptions; they are divorced from them. But it matters from what they got divorced.

We do not know the name of St. Mark's youth, nor of the Master of the Aix Annunciation. Yet we can refer to them, and rigidly at that, by means of these descriptions. Thus names are not indispensable. Still, think of the horrors of doing history, geography, or simple gossiping, without proper names . . . They are indeed the skeleton of our referring apparatus.

To sum up: if speaker A wishes to refer to individual S in talking to listener B, then A has to express, in the form of a definite noun-phrase, such a subset of elements from the estimated overlap between their representations of S as he regards sufficient in the given situation to cause B to think of S.

13. If there is no estimated overlap, that is to say, if the speaker has no reason to think that the individual he wishes to talk about is known to

the hearer, or if he does not know in what terms he is known, then, as we suggested above, he can remedy the deficiency by introducing that individual to the listener himself.

The purpose of such an introduction is to create a representation in the listener's mind causally linked to his own image of that individual, which in turn is derived, firsthand, second-hand, or no hand, from the individual itself, if there is such in reality. Since we are primarily concerned with linguistic communication, the image thus created will be · a conceptual construction evoked by means of an indefinite description supplied by the speaker. Some examples:

> A student came into the office this morning . . .
> Kant had a servant . . .
> Once upon a time there was a king . . .
> Hercules choked a lion . . .

Once the introduction is performed, the speaker may go on to refer to the individual in question, since, *ipso facto*, he can be sure of the existence and of the nature of the listener's representation. Thus he can proceed, e.g.

> *He* was all upset about *his* grade . . .
> *His* name was Lampe . . .
> *The king* had seven daughters . . .
> . . . and carried *him* to his master . . .

For the same reason, once the introduction is made, the listener too can refer to those individuals:

> What was *his* name?
> What happened to *the lion*?

The definite noun-phrases in these sentences are, of course, anaphorically related to the sentences used in the introduction. This fact lends support to the idea, which I put forward in an earlier paper, that even in the cases in which a definite description is used without introduction, it is anaphorically related to a proposition which the speaker assumes to be known to the addressee, as part of his representation of the individual the speaker intends to talk about.[15] Think of 'the girl who arrived late last night'. The speaker assumes that her late arrival last night also pertains to the listener's image of that girl. In this case,

---

[15] 'Singular Terms' in my *Linguistics in Philosophy*. See also my *Res Cogitans*, particularly pp. 73–8.

however, that proposition is not expressed in the discourse, since no introduction is needed. But what if the listener comes to think of another girl, who arrived still later, unbeknownst to the speaker? Well, then, there is a case of misunderstanding. The "estimated overlap" was not strong enough. Still, the speaker did refer, happily though unsuccessfully, to the girl of *his* choice.

If the resulting image in the listener's mind is entirely due to the speaker's introduction, then there is no danger of a misunderstanding on this score. For, as we remember, the power of unique denotation is not due to the descriptive content, but to the causal link. And this is assured by the speaker's intention. Therefore, even if, say, seven students came into my office this morning, my words, 'A student came into my office this morning', will create an image in your mind *of* the student I have in mind in saying these words. And the subsequent reference, made by you or me, will be to *him*.

We may recall that, in the cases of ostension, introduction and reference may go hand in hand, executed in one move. The phrase *that man*, accompanied by a suitable gesture, can introduce and refer at the same time. This possibility is not restricted to ostensive situations; think of the use of phrases like *my father*, *Caesar's wife*, or *Kant's servant*. The relations by means of which the introduction is made suggest uniqueness (although more in the first case than in the others), so it is possible to incorporate them into the referring phrase. Not so if the relation is more open. *My brother* sits more comfortably if I have only one brother, and *my student* won't do, unless I am known as a private tutor to a young lord or something like that. Normally, as we just saw, I have to introduce the particular student I have in mind. To use a definite description, finally, for the purposes of introduction in such a situation would create a misunderstanding: the listener would assume that the individual has already been introduced to him. If I begin with 'The student who came into my office this morning', you will ask 'Which student?'

We often introduce individuals by name. If a small child asks me 'Who discovered America?', my answer may be 'Columbus'. And if *you* ask me 'Who discovered Trinidad?', my answer might be the same, 'Columbus'. Yet, I think, I introduce Columbus in the first case, and refer to him in the second. For I assume that you, but not the child, know of Columbus. Indeed, a more complete answer to the child's question would be this: 'A man called Christopher Columbus'. Such an answer would be out of place to your question.

14. Christ has suffered under Pontius Pilate—so holds the Creed, which little Johnny had to memorize. Thus, when asked by his teacher to draw the scene of the Crucifixion, he put an aeroplane into the picture, just above the Cross, with Pontius Pilot in it. Did he indeed draw that illustrious magistrate? He got his name wrong (did he?), and just about everything else. Yet there is some reason to think that he did draw Pilate: 'He thought Pilate was a pilot, the funny boy!' one might say. For, after all, it was the Creed, an impeccable pedigree, that caused his image of Pilate—albeit again in a funny way.

But did he, or didn't he? I don't exactly know. Our theory, stretched to the breaking point, cannot decide. It would be a poor recommendation for it if it could.

V

Being There

1. LET US recall the representation of the world we considered at the end of Chapter I. We projected the universe extended in space and time, and containing all the things that common experience and science reveals in it. Among these things there are some organisms which claim our attention as anchors of transference, which we recognize in other words as sentient beings, subjects of experience. One of these organisms is my own body, the seat of the consciousness I actually enjoy, the residence of my mind. Yet, as we remember, this body and this mind have no privileged status; they make up but one conscious being among the many, equal or comparable. The fact, moreover, that I am this being rather than some other does not belong to this representation; the designation that I am this thing escapes even the most complete description of the world. For even if I were not Z.V. but, say, Richard M. Nixon, it would remain the same world, the same Vendler, the same Nixon, without a change. The fact that I am Z.V., if it is one, is not a fact about the world.

Yet, no doubt, I am that thing: I am Z.V., and not Napoleon, Nixon, or that cat. And this is not an empty claim, no mere instance of the truism that everything is what it is and not something else. For although the fact that I am Z.V. rather than Richard Nixon makes no difference to the world, it makes all the difference to *me*. I can imagine what it must be like being Nixon, and it surely is different from being Z.V. Accordingly, if I were Nixon, I would be in a different condition, even if the world would not. And when I am glad, or sad, that I am not he, these sentiments are not provoked by the trivial fact that Vendler is not Nixon, that one thing is not another thing. It would be silly indeed for me to be happy or distressed about the fact that, for example, Jerry Ford is not Richard Nixon, but it is by no means silly to be glad that I am not.

In the same way, when I feel content with being who·I am, my satisfaction is not due to the triviality that Z.V. is identical with him-self; and if I feel a desire to have lived the life of Napoleon rather than my own, the object of this desire is certainly not the impossible identity of Z.V. and Napoleon. 'I wish I had been Napoleon' does not mean 'I wish Napoleon and Vendler were the same'.

The same point can be made by taking a leaf out of Leibniz's book. God contemplates the plan of the best world, which lies open to him, revealing all details, including the complete individual concepts of all creatures. Yet not even this unsurpassable *Who's Who* will contain any information as to who I am. 'My Lord,' I ask him, 'this is a great world indeed, but what concerns me most is where I will fit into it; which individual· concept will be mine?' 'I cannot tell you that;' answers God 'that you'll have to find out for yourself.' And he speaks the truth, for although what this "veil of ignorance" hides escapes even divine omniscience, it can be found out and known by me alone.

Moreover, if I am so inclined, I can be grateful, and praise God for having wrought such a lovely world, containing Vendler, Napoleon, Nixon, and the rest, but it makes no sense to praise or blame him for the fact that I happen to be this man and not those. Yet this fact, to me, is no less important than the goodness or badness of the world at large.

Thus, the proposition that I am Z.V. is not the same as the tautology that Z.V. is Z.V., and the proposition that I am not Napoleon is not the same as the trivial truth that Z.V. is not Napoleon. How is, then, this proposition, 'I am Z.V.', to be understood.[1]

2. 'Well,' you suggest, 'look at the way in which such sentences are used, to begin with.' This is good advice; let us see indeed. I use that sentence quite frequently, and there seems to be no mystery about its role. Given the results of our reflections on reference, and particularly what we said about Columbus at the end, it is quite clear that I can use that sentence to achieve two different aims.

The first of these is to introduce myself. It is a social convention in

---

[1] In the last two decades or so the peculiarities of "I-statements" have been the subject of an extensive literature. Castañeda, Anscombe, Perry, Lewis, and Chisholm, among others, contributed to the discussion, illuminating certain aspects and offering various solutions (I list some of their papers in the Bibliography). I have neither the inclination nor the space to make a survey of these views and compare them with mine. As far as I can see, however, none of these positions considers statements like 'I am Z.V.' against the background of imaginary transference, i.e. the possibility of being someone else. My main concern is with the epistemological, or rather transcendental, grounds for such statements, which express one's location in a "centreless" world-representation, rather than with their mere logical form.

our culture that when person A, who is unknown to person B, meets B for the first time, A gets introduced, or introduces himself. And this last task is normally discharged by A's telling his name to B. Why his name? For the reasons we explained above: in order to be sure that B's representation of him contains this item, which is the most suitable device for any reference B might wish to make to him in the future.

There may be some special situations in which the same purpose can be served by mentioning some other particular: nickname, assumed name, serial number, title, and so forth. 'I am the Secretary to the President' will do, for example, if that is the only context in which the speaker expects the hearer to remember him and to refer to him in the days to come.

In any case, however, whether the introduction is performed by giving a name or some other particular, what the speaker tells the addressee is nothing but a contingent fact about himself; an especially useful item to be added to the hearer's emerging image of the same. 'I am Z.V.' in this context means the same as, and indeed can be replaced by, 'I am called Z.V.' or 'My name is Z.V.' Needless to say, I might have been baptized differently, or have acquired another name, in which case that name would be mentioned in performing introductions.

But there is another way in which such a sentence as 'I am Z.V.' can be used, namely not to introduce, but to identify oneself. In these situations the speaker assumes that he is already known to the addressee by that name. Suppose I am told at a philosophy convention that a certain person whom I never met before is looking for me, say, to recommend a graduate student. When I am taken to him, I say 'I am Z.V.' Now, in this case it would be misleading to say that what that person just learned is my name; no, what he just learned is who I am. And this is quite another thing.

For consider, once more, a simple introduction. A person to whom I was totally unknown is standing before me and, presumably, forms an "image" of me in his mind. What he learns in talking to me, including my name, progressively fills up that representation. Now, the person whom I meet at the convention also sees me as I approach, and forms an image of me in his mind. But this person already has another representation of me in his memory: he has heard of me before, may have read something I wrote, and the like. Thus my words, 'I am Z.V.', do not merely add something to his present image, but also connect it with the other one he already has, by virtue of the name which belongs to both. 'So this man (. . . in front of me . . .) is that man (. . . who wrote . . .)' he might conclude, expressing the *identity* of the source of two representations. And since, as we saw, those two representations are necessarily tied to me by causal links, what he comes to realize is a necessary truth.

In the example I just gave I intended this result, since I knew that that person had been looking for *me*. In some cases what is meant to be a simple introduction may have the same effect. I might not know, in introducing myself, that the person already knows about me by name.

Names, as we remarked above, have a special role in these matters, but by no means an exclusive one. As one can be introduced by other means, so can one be identified. 'I am the teacher who failed you in Logic at Cornell' might identify me in my past victim's mind even better than my name. For, as he has forgotten my appearance, he may not remember the name either. But, owing to that grade, he most probably remembers *me*.

3. All introductions are aimed, therefore, at acquainting the addressee with a feature of the subject—name or some other suitable attribute—to bring about recognition, or to facilitate future reference to him. The speaker may be a third person, or the subject himself. In the former case the speaker finds this feature in his own image of the subject. And in the latter case? Obviously, the speaker draws upon his own self-image. After all, in order to introduce myself, I must know my name, or some other thing about myself, which I mention to that purpose.

Of course you can be wrong in your image of me, but so can I. One's own self-representation is by no means infallible. There are madmen who think they are Napoleon, and there was a housewife in New Jersey or some place who believed she was Princess Anastasia, the daughter of the last Czar. And, to recall an old story, if I had been stolen by gypsies as an infant, then, in a sense, I would not know my true identity, my "individual essence", as it were, which consists in my origins. For that matter, few of us can be absolutely sure about these things—babies do get switched in maternity wards. Not to speak of victims of amnesia, hypnosis, or science-fiction set-ups—so beloved by some philosophers—involving brain-transplants, computer attachments, brain-in-tank horrors, and the like. By the way, do not forget Descartes and his demon either.

Yet I surely know something when I reflect on my identity; maybe

I am wrong about my name, my provenance, and my past, but I still know that I am *this* person and not another, not you I am talking to, or that woman in the corner. 'But the demon may be deceiving you,' warns Descartes's ghost, 'there may be no man, no body that is.' Be that as it may, I reply, I still have a representation of this body and this mind, one among the many in the world, which I claim to be mine. And when I introduce or describe myself, it is this representation, right or wrong, that provides the data. But these data, then, belong to the image of the world I conjured up a while ago; that this thing is called Z.V., that it taught Logic at Cornell, that it sits at this desk writing these lines, are all facts belonging to a complete description of the world. If so, then whatever I may know *about* this person will still not comprise the fact that I *am* this individual. For that fact cannot pertain to the description of the world.

4. When you introduce or identify me you have to refer to me by the use of an indexical or some other suitable device. '*This* is Z.V.,' you might say, or '*He* is the one who failed you at Cornell.' When I introduce myself I use the word *I* to the same purpose. *I*, therefore, functions as an indexical in a speech-act, denoting the speaker: 'I am Z.V.' means, for instance, 'The person who is saying these words is called Z.V.' But this piece of information sheds no light on the problem of my identity either, for it leaves out the crucial fact that *I* am the person who is saying these words. Then why don't I say this: 'I am the person who is saying these words'? Because, obviously, it would be redundant in any conversation, whereas 'I am Z.V.' is not. And the reason is that, according to what we just said about the use of *I* in speech-acts, the former sentence would mean that the person who is saying those words is the person who is saying those words, but the latter conveys the useful information that the person saying those words is called Z.V. This is how things look from your point of view, from which I am just another feature of your environment. But for me, this is by no means the end of the story; for me, the sentence 'I am the one who is saying these words' does contain a crucial piece of information, which, in fact, is sufficient to locate me in the world. Thus the *I* in these sentences, as I myself understand them, has a double burden to bear. I use it to refer to myself as a subject, and, as an indexical, to refer to myself as an object in the world.[2]

Consider the passage taken from a (fictional) horror-story. 'And as

[2] Frege holds a similar view in 'The Thought: a Logical Inquiry'.

I saw the monster slowly approaching I heard a scream. I looked around and came to realize that it was I who uttered the scream . . . ' The last occurrence of *I* in this text functions differently from the previous three. Speaking in the first person (i.e. as if I were that character), I explain the difference as follows. With the first three occurrences of *I*, I attribute certain conscious things directly to *me*, as a subject, and only directly to *it*, (this thing in the world). With the last occurrence I attribute the screaming (unconscious) directly to *it*, and only indirectly to *me*. The question remains: how is it that this "it" is, in one sense, "I"?[3]

A computer can print out, or even say, 'I do not know the answer', and we understand what it says: the *I* it utters is nothing but an indexical referring to itself. But the *I* for the machine has no other role to play: there is no subject for whom the sentence 'I am this machine' would be significant; there is no subject who could find himself in that machine.

Thus the role which statements like 'I am Z.V.' play in the "language game" does not illuminate the mystery of one's identity. That game, as any other game, is played in the world, and its rules say nothing about the question: which of the players am I?

5. But, perhaps, my self-image is singled out by its completeness or richness of detail? Don't I know more about myself than about any other conscious being?

Unfortunately, this is not necessarily so, either. It is quite possible to imagine a set-up in which I would know more about somebody else than about myself. Suppose I am a victim of a terrible accident; I come to my senses paralysed from the neck down, lying in an iron lung, in a state of total amnesia about my past life. I have no idea who I am, or what I look like. A kind nurse, whom I see clearly since I am not blind, tells me about her life to while away the empty hours. After a few days of this, I certainly will know more about her than about myself. I may wish I were she, healthy and happy as she is—but I am not. I am linked to the universe via this wrecked body and empty mind; this is what I am—but what does this mean?

[3] In a similar way, the sudden realization that, e.g. the seedy looking character I see in the department store mirror is I, or that the person who is spilling sugar on the floor is I (see Perry, 1979), is nothing but the discovery of some unexpected aspect pertaining to *this man*, i.e. Z.V., who I am. These cases are no different from recognizing myself in an old photograph, or in an X-ray picture. None of these discoveries affect the basic fact that I am this man (with all his appearances) and not somebody else who I can imagine being.

Nothing but the following: my actual experiences correspond to the projected experiences of that body. Lying there in the iron lung I imagine myself as I am—an exercise of objective imagination. I see myself in that sorry state, and focus my attention on the condition of my body: the broken neck, the injured spinal cord, the position of the head, the perspective of the eyes. Then I switch tracks and pursue the subjective path of fancy: try to imagine what it must be like being in that state. What it must feel like lying like that; how the machine, the room and the nurse must appear from that point of view; what her voice must sound like, and so on. And, of course, that is what I do see if I open my eyes, that is what I feel and hear in actuality. Then this is my body, and the experiences I am having pertain to my mind. That other person, the nurse, though better known to me in body and in mind—I see her and share her memories—is not I, is not the person who I am. She closes her eyes and behold, I still see the room; she looks at me, and I do not see my head.

Thus my identity is a matter of access: I am this man, I am Z.V., because the experiences I have fit into the pattern of the projected experiences of this man; in other words, I am Z.V. because it is his experiences to which I have a privileged access.[4]

6. As we may recall, there is an affinity between the data of perception and the representations produced by the imagination. This is shown by such mixed tasks as viewing one's wife in the dress seen in the shop window, trying to find a suitable place on the wall for a picture, etc.

Still more important, in recognizing or simply perceiving an object for what it is, the deliveries of the senses have to be integrated into a representation of that object evoked in imagination. To recognize a lamp, for instance, is to fit some perceived features into a pattern projectible for a lamp. For the mere notion of a lamp, by itself, shows no such affinity: concepts and intuitions do not mix. Yet there is no fixed image associated with the concept that could do the trick: no image can capture all the perspectives in which lamps may appear. What is needed is a schema determined by or associated with the concept, which enables the imagination to evoke a picture into which the actual perceptions can be integrated. As we noted in Chapter I, the working of the imagination in this respect is not unlike that of

---

[4] This view gives content to Frege's claim: 'Now everyone is presented to himself in a particular and primitive way, in which he is presented to no-one else' ('The Thought', p. 25).

a computer, which, given the data of, say, a regular solid, is able to project its appearance, in whole or in part, from a desired perspective on its screen. To see a lamp, then, is to be aware of an appearance which the imagination represents as belonging to a lamp. This is how sensory intuition gets converted into objective perception.

Returning now to the business of one's own identity, the situation is strictly analogous. One becomes aware of oneself by fitting one's current experiences into the pattern projected by the imagination— now along the subjective path—as pertaining to one particular body. I am Z.V., because what I am feeling and perceiving now is what Z.V. ought to feel and perceive at this moment. And in this way, again, the subjective "I" is converted into the person Z.V., one of the sentient beings of the universe. Thus, when I feel cold now, it is Z.V. who feels cold, sitting in a cold room.

'But the current state of my consciousness is much richer in content than anything I could project on the basis of the known condition of my body,' you object. 'This stab of pain in my tooth, this tickle on my scalp, the feeling of irritation that I have—I am not aware of any foundation for these perceptions and sentiments in my known bodily state. Yet, no doubt, these too belong to me.'

They do indeed, I reply. Because, in the first place, they occur in time. Nothing, however, can be so perceived which is not related to objective processes, i.e. to series of events distinct from and independent of my perceiving them. Now, the changes of my body, and of its physical environment, are, *de facto*, the objective processes to which I relate all the experiences I can have, whether or not they are such as can be connected to some known condition of my body. The stab of pain I just felt in my tooth occurred after I lifted my head to look out the window, and before I started writing this sentence.

Sensations, moreover, are normally felt in the body, even if we are aware of no stimulation to account for them. And, more important, they can be influenced by manipulations affecting the body. Even pains due to unknown causes may be alleviated by taking aspirin. *Mutatis mutandis* the same thing holds true of emotions: they, too, often show bodily symptoms, and there are physical means of modifying them—well known to bar-tenders and the drug industry.

In these matters, too, the parallel between being aware of one's mind and perceiving physical objects holds true. To see a lamp is a richer experience than just perceiving what a lamp of that kind ought to look like. The work of the imagination, guided by concepts and schemata, is bound to fall short of the data of experience, yet it makes objective experience what it is. For all the details provided by sensation are to be fitted into the spatial confines of that object, otherwise they would not belong to it at all.

And, for the same reason, all the subjective experiences one has are to be placed in the temporal sequence of inner events inseparably tied to the known processes of one's body. Otherwise, to use Kant's words, such experiences would be "nothing to us".

Why do we pinch ourselves in some queer situations? To be sure that what we perceive constitutes real experience. As the clapboard in the film-studio is used to coordinate sight and sound, so the pinch, a bodily event with a clear mental counterpart, serves to anchor the surrounding perceptions into time and reality.

7. Thus there is a difference—not in content, but in origin—between the representation of one's own mind and the representation of another mind. The latter is entirely due to the work of the imagination based on our knowledge of the conditions of another body. There is that man, for instance, behaving in a certain manner, and perhaps uttering certain words. By performing transference I can imagine being in that state, and thus represent his experiences. Accordingly, the only access I have to his mind is based on the observable state of his body.

In my own case, there is another source: the content of my actual experience exceeds the projected experiences of my known bodily state. To put it simply, there are features of my current experience that are not captured by merely imagining being in the bodily state I know myself to be. My sitting in this chair, in this room, writing these lines, etc., do not account for the slight headache I have. This fact is behind the doctrine of the "privileged access", and this is the point of Descartes's remarks about the sailor and his ship.[5]

Yet, as we just remarked, even these features are to be integrated into *my* state of mind, i.e. into the state of mind projectible for this particular body. Since, moreover, these experiences are of the same kind as, and are indeed contiguous with, the ones I can project, the natural assumption is the following: there must be a bodily condition, maybe unknown, but certainly knowable, which would account for these experiences too. In the given case there must be a nervous condition responsible for my headache. This assumption, of course, is familiar to us from Chapter II. In dealing with the problem of inverted spectra

[5] In *Meditation Six*.

and related matters, we came to the conclusion that the features of inner life must be determined by bodily conditions. It is interesting to note that this result, which we established on transcendental grounds, appears in the so-called "identity theory" in scientific disguise.

According to what we said in the previous section, a similar observation can be made concerning the perception of our environment. Direct observation reveals more than can be projected in imagining an object known to us. And, again, since even these features are to be integrated into that projection to become part of that real thing, we postulate physical causes to account for them. There must be a tiny crack in that lamp to account for the faint black line I perceive.

To conclude, once more: I am the creature to whose mind I have a privileged access.

8. Thomas Nagel[6] and some of the authors mentioned in footnote 1 of this chapter, draw an analogy between the designation of the "I" among the sentient creatures in the world, and the designation of the "now" among the moments of time in objective history.

This comparison is apt and illuminating. As there is nothing in the image of the world that would single out the self, there is nothing in the same space-time representation which would pick out the present moment. Yet it is true that now it is 10 a.m. (GMT), 1 December 1979 (abbreviated henceforth as 10-1-12-79). And, as the statement that I am Z.V. is not an empty claim of self-identity, neither is the claim that now is 10-1-12-79. 'Thank God, my headache is over' does not express my satisfaction with the triviality that the headacheless 10-1-12-79 is later than the headacheful 9-1-12-79 in the representation of the world, but voices my relief that the "now" is located at the less painful point.[7]

Dulcis est memoria malorum praeteritorum; yet those *mala* were by no means *dulcia* when they occurred. Similarly, a threat of a whipping to come in five minutes is a far more upsetting prospect than of one to

---

[6] In *The Possibility of Altruism*.

[7] Above we remarked that it makes no sense to thank God for being this man rather than some other. In a similar way, it makes no sense to thank God for being at this point of time rather than an earlier or a later one. Accordingly, whereas God may be praised for making that headache short or bearable, he cannot sensibly be praised for the fact that it is over *now*. For one thing, as God cannot know who *I* am, he cannot know what time it is *now*. He, the omniscient and omnipotent God, has nothing to do with either of these "indexical" facts.

be inflicted ten years hence. 'But,' you ask, 'why is the prospect of future evil more disturbing than the memory of past evil?' Well, for one thing, because you cannot do anything about the past, but your actions can influence the future. And your anxiety about the future is a healthy stimulus to do something about it. At any rate, to repeat an expression we used before: whether something is past, present, or future, makes no difference to the world; but to me it makes all the difference.

In the previous sections of this chapter we gave a solution for the problem of finding the self in terms of satisfaction of imaginary expectations. Is there a similar way of locating the "now"?

It is a matter of giving a finer account of the very same solution. The person Z.V., whom I singled out as me, is an entity extended in space and time. Consequently the imaginary expectations we just mentioned stretch out over time. My experiences of yesterday correspond to the vicissitudes my body underwent yesterday, as today's experiences mirror the history of the same body today. Now, yesterday's events are preserved in my memory in two ways: as memory of propositions, and as memory of experience. I remember that I walked on the beach yesterday, and I remember walking on the beach. You can remember the first thing too, since it is an objective fact, part of the history of the world, but only I can recall the second. Now, I know that I am the person who walked on the beach yesterday because the content of my subjective memory corresponds to the projected experiences of that person, whom I can represent walking there, on the basis of my memory of facts. In general: I am the person whose history is mirrored in my subjective memory.

The important point to retain is this: I find myself not in my subjective states, remembered or experienced, but in the objective world, as a constituent of that manifold represented in the imagination. Yet it is by means of those subjective states that I find myself: for they fulfil the imaginary expectations raised by the history of that particular organism.

And in the same way the "now", the present moment, is to be placed in the objective time-sequence of the world. For the "now", as contrasted with the past and the future, makes sense only in the order of time. As my experiences do not contain the "I", they do not contain the "now" either as an inherent feature; they are timelessly given, to be dated and timed in relation to the objective processes of the world. This is the reason why we are unable to say how long the present experiences (the "spacious present") last. But, of course, once they are dated, they belong to the past. This is the paradox of the "now": as subjective experience it is not in time, and once placed in time, it is part of past history: as one cannot "catch" the "I", one cannot "catch" the present moment either.

But how is it that a certain portion of objective time is perceived as past, and the rest is expected as future? We said above that I am the man whose subjective memory matches the imaginary expectations warranted by the history of my body. It is by virtue of this correlation that remembered experiences are placed in time. For they do not carry any dates either. The vicarious experience of recalling walking on the beach does not contain any information about the date of that walk; it has to be supplied *ex aliunde* by fitting it into the history of my life—and the history of that beach. We remember dreams, too. But can we date the events they contain?

Now, the memory of past experience coexists with current perceptions: I recall walking on the beach while consciously sitting at my desk. Which set of experiences are the memory, and which the current bunch? Well, the current perceptions fit my actual state, since, in fact, I am sitting at the desk now. So the "now" returns like a yet untamed beast. But at least I know that this state is later than that walk on the beach; that is a fact of objective history. This, however, is clearly not enough for calling it the present state. Last night's supper was later too, and today's lunch to come is later still.

Yes, but I do not recall today's lunch, as I recall that walk, nor do I experience it as I do my sitting at this desk. I anticipate it, however, and may form vivid expectations concerning its likely content and circumstance. That I call something memory, current experience, or expectation, however, is a function of the "now" already fixed. For both the processes of my body and my mental states go through them in the same way, without pausing for a "now".

Above, in connection with pinning down the self, we happened upon the fact of a privileged access I enjoy with respect to my own states. Now, clearly, I do have such an access to the present and the past. My current experiences are richer than the experiences my imagination would project given the known condition of my body. This holds true of past experiences too: in recalling a face, a voice, a smell, or an emotion, I experience more than what could be projected on the basis of my knowledge of the circumstances involved. By merely imagining what a certain book might have smelled like, I do not capture the particular experience I so vividly recall.

With respect to the future, however, I do not have a privileged access. My memories of that walk on the beach do not depend upon the reconstruction of the physical set-up: they are given independently, to be integrated in objective history. But my projection of the experiences of today's lunch are entirely dependent upon my expectations of the objective circumstances of that meal: where it will take place, what I shall eat, and the like. Thus, in this case, I am no better off than in imagining the experiences of somebody else. With respect to the past, proximate or remote, there are two paths to my mental state: imaginary projection, and memory of experience; what it must have been like walking on the beach, and what it was like walking on the beach. In regard to the future, however, only the first route is available: I can imagine what it will be like eating those mussels for lunch; but there is no such thing as "retro-remembering" eating them now, via a special access to my future. In one word: I have a privileged access to my past, but not to my future. And the "now" is the forward limit of my objective history covered by the privileged access.

9. The privileged access to one's past is matched by an equally special relation to one's future.

As I just suggested, we can, to some extent at least, predict the future, and, by means of the imagination, anticipate our experiences. Will it rain tonight? How do I go about answering this question? Well, by considering the condition of the atmosphere, as far as it is known to me from my own observations and from the weather-report read in the papers. Given this, and my knowledge of meteorology, I make the prediction: it is very likely that it will, because . . . , and I mention certain facts, if you are interested. Thus I make the forecast on the basis of my representation of this part of the universe.

Shall I go out tonight, even if it rains? Now this question is a horse of a different colour. Do I look for an answer in my representation of the world; of the neuro-physiological state of this man, Z.V., in particular? Not at all: I will go out, if I so decide, and never mind the fine details of my physiology. And if you ask me why, I may tell you about the interesting show I want to see.

Thus, as there is a privileged access to my current and past states, which is independent of the representation of my body, so there is a privileged agency found in me, which is independent of the causal processes I recognize in the same representation. And as the domain of the privileged access is the past up to the present, so the domain of privileged agency is the future beginning with the present. One more similarity: the privileged access is restricted to the experiences projectible for a certain body; the privileged agency is confined to the movements of the same body. As I cannot experience sitting in this chair without my body, so I cannot move this chair without moving my body.

Of course, this agency is by no means omnipotent. I can move the chair but not the house, can walk but not fly. But these restrictions. are entailed by my representation of the same body: it is an organism, a machine, if you like, of limited power and tolerance. In this respect, again, there is no essential difference between me and you, or between me and an ant, elephant, or motorcar. Except, of course, that the motorcar does not encourage transference. But you do, and since you are a human being, in imagining being you, I imagine being a free agent once more.

Now suppose I decide to push that chair, and I move my hand to do so. I experience the visual and kinaesthetic sensations of that move, and, accordingly, the movement of that hand will appear in my self-representation. Now, obviously, this event is by no means an exceptional occurrence in the history of the world; it has to be integrated into the causal network of the universe, to be explained in physiological, neurological, thus ultimately in physical terms, like any other event. But what if I had not pushed the chair, but raised my hand instead? After all, I could have done so. Well, in that case the going up of my hand would have to be accounted for in terms of contracting muscles, stimulated motor-nerves, certain processes in the central nervous system, and so forth. In that case, therefore, my total representation of the universe would be somewhat different from what it is now. The point is that the exercise of my freedom does not appear as a causal factor in my representation of the world. For that image is a function of my past experience; and free agency, as such, does not appear in it. What *I* brought about shows up as an event neatly integrated into the causal network of the whole.

There is nothing strange in this. The world is as it is, to a small extent at least, because of what I, and other free agents, have done in the past. Had we acted differently, the world would be different. Yet in no case would it be a world with loose ends and holes in its causal network.

'This may take care of the past,' you object, 'but what about the future? Is it not the case that your representation of the world

determines the future course of your body's history? And if so, how
can you be free now to lift your arm or not?'

My answer is as follows. My image of the world is a function of what
I am experiencing now, what I remember, and what I know about the
world. Now none of these sources contains anything that would be
incompatible with my arm's going up in the next moment. I am not
paralysed, not in shackles, and so forth. Therefore my self-representation
is indifferent in this respect.

'But wait,' you insist, 'don't you know that the universe is such that
its state at time t_1 determines its later state at t_2? Now you are at t_1.
Ergo . . . '

Yes indeed, I answer, I do know that if I lift my arm at t_2, then at
that time I shall have to represent my body and the world at t_1 in such
a manner as to account for my arm's going up at t_2. This does not
mean, however, that I have to represent it so now.

There is a set of world pictures, W_1, in which Z.V.'s arm goes up at
t_2, and there is another set, W_2, in which it does not. Let us assume now
that at time t_1 my experiences, memories, etc. are compatible with
either group. At t_2 I raise my arm on set purpose. Then I know that
a member of W_1 represents the real world. And it is my doing that it
does.

Each of these pictures is causally complete and has no room for a
free or outside agency. And my freedom does not consist in tinkering
with these representations. The effect of my decision is to narrow the
choice among them.

10. You are still entitled to a parting shot, however, and it comes forth
in this form: 'But what if you did have a complete access to the current
microscopic state of your body, and, through the interconnectedness of
all things, to the present time-slice of the cosmos, together with a full
mastery of the laws of nature? In that case, in the manner of Laplace's
demon, you could predict what you body will *de facto* do, and there
would be no room left for free choice. I know, of course, that physicists
would not countenance this possibility, but I do not think that your
argument hinges on their objections.'

It does not, I answer. And in the main point, too, I agree with you.
In that case there would be no freedom—but there would be no "I"
or "now" either. For in that case I would not have a privileged access
to the state of any particular organism, and, accordingly, there could
be no latter end in time to such access. If I knew absolutely everything

about the physiological states of all organisms at all times, then my projection of their mental states would be complete, and would leave no room for a privileged access. Then everything would be out in the open, and I would have the same relation to all organisms, both as to their objective and subjective states, and equally to all points in their temporal history. I would be some sort of deity, in other words, omnipresent in space and time.

Thus it is essential for my identity, my location in time, and my freedom, that I do not have an exhaustive representation of myself in the world, so that I can have a special relation to the subjective states, and the future history, of one particular body.

11. In the earlier sections of this chapter I insisted upon the integration of the delivery of one's privileged access into the texture of one's world representation; both objectively, i.e. in assigning them to objects, and subjectively, i.e. in fitting them into the imaginary expectations raised by the condition of a certain organism. Later on, however, we stressed the need of suiting one's world image to the data of experience, or even of selecting among rival representations.

Indeed, it is quite obvious that the connection between the representation of the world, including one's own body, on the one hand, and the delivery of one's experience, on the other, has to be a two-way street. For that representation is by no means a fixed, finished, and unalterable picture. To begin with, it is no doubt more full in regions covering the spatio-temporal vicinity of one's body, more rich in macroscopic than in microscopic detail, and so forth. Furthermore, as we just saw, it is more definite about the past than about the future, notwithstanding the fact that the picture, in itself, has no way of demarcating the two.

With the growth of one's knowledge, whether obtained by learning or by one's own experience, the picture will sharpen and acquire more detail. To put it in another way, the available alternatives will diminish. When a doubt is resolved, a set of alternatives is eliminated.

Alternative representations have another role to play, however, in one's speculations about possible states: about what might have been, or may yet come. Even if I know that Hitler has lost World War II, I may consider what would have happened up to now, and would yet come about, if he had won.

In all these speculations, however, I remain passive, i.e. do not consider interfering myself with the contemplated course of events.

But, of course, I may plan to interfere, to act, that is, and thereby steer the course of history in one direction rather than another. Now, I can do nothing about the past, except to regret or to rejoice. But the future is open in this respect. The present moment, then, from this point of view, appears to be the beginning of the stretch of time in which some events at least are to be determined by the free agency I enjoy over my body.

Thus, to complete the parallel drawn above, as the "now" is the end of my privileged access to my bodily states, so it is the beginning of my free disposal over the same body. I am *at* a certain point of the space-time universe anchored in a body by the double links of privileged access and free disposal, the temporal domains of which relations meet in the "now".

VI

The Transcendental Self

A. SUBJECT OF TRANSFERENCE

1. AS the title of this chapter indicates, the time has come to display and examine the main implication of this whole essay in a direct and uncompromising fashion. The view I propose, a doctrine of the transcendental self, is bound to be unpopular, or worse, in the present climate of "reductionist" psychology and philosophy of mind. Since, however, at least in my estimate, no other approach has been able to provide a coherent solution for the inter-connected problems of subjectivity, other minds, and freedom, dictates of fashion should not be allowed to bar the avenue that promises an adequate account.

The idea of the transcendental self is due to Kant. Moreover, as the reader must have realized by this time, I have been inspired by his work in many ways. Yet, I do not regard this essay as a piece of Kant interpretation. I merely employ some of his ideas, as far as I understand them, for my own purposes, without, however, claiming the sanction of his authority for my results. Should it turn out, nevertheless, that some of my observations still cast a light on his doctrine here and there, then I would regard this as a gratuitous boon.

I shall not worry, therefore, about reductionists on the one hand, and Kant-scholars on the other, in what I am going to say. Another aspect of the forthcoming discussion, however, fills me with unease and trepidation. Talking about the transcendental self is like talking about God: our natural concepts are not designed to carry such a burden; they are stretched to the breaking point, yet we have nothing better to replace them. Thus, one compromises: unable to say what these things really are, one tries at least to say what they are like, but only to find again that the analogies offered are misleading, and require disclaimers cancelling out some unwanted implications. I shall assert, for instance, that the transcendental self is a subject, but it is not something that can be named or described; that it exists, but not in any possible world; that it determines causal chains, without itself being a cause; etc. What, then, is the point of carrying on like this? It is to show that there are some specific reasons for trying to say certain things beyond what can be clearly stated; to show that the empirical world, as perceived by a subject, points beyond itself, in spite of the fact that it is perceived as complete. If so, then speaking in parables may be better than remaining silent, and seeing *per speculum in aenigmate* better than not looking at all.

2. I first alluded to the notion of a transcendental self at the end of Chapter II—just to be dropped as something too hot to handle at that stage.

The idea, as we recall, has arisen as follows. We came to realize that in performing transference, i.e. in imagining being someone else, the object of the exercise cannot be fancying *me* (Z.V.) being identical with that person. In imagining, for instance, being Ronald Reagan, I cannot be imagining the identity of Z.V. with R.R., for it is patently impossible for these two men to be one and the same, and the patently impossible cannot be imagined. Therefore we concluded, following the Voice of Reason, that imagining, say, being R.R. must simply consist in fancying being in a certain possible state, without involving Z.V. in the object of the exercise.

So far so good. But, as we noted at that time, a nagging worry remains. In imagining being R.R. I conjure up something which is not the case. What is not the case? That I am in fact R.R. Now this "I" cannot mean Z.V., since in doing this transference I do not imagine Z.V. to be R.R.; what I do imagine is that *I* am R.R. Therefore, it seems, "I", the subject of this act, is not identical with Z.V. Yet, no doubt, it is Z.V. who performs the act . . . What, then, is the relation between this "I", and Z.V., if not identity?

The solution may lie in a phrase we used a few lines back. Being R.R., we said, is being in a possible "state". Accordingly, imagining being he, I fancy being in that state. If so, then, obviously, being Z.V. is being in another state. To put it bluntly, the statement 'I am Z.V.' may mean that I am in the state of being Z.V. In reflecting upon this statement in the previous chapter we remarked that it has a sense, not as you understand it but as I do, which expresses my "presence" in the world: where I am, at which point I am anchored in the texture of the universe. To be thus located, then, in this body and with this mind, is to be in the state of being Z.V.

For the purposes of greater clarity in this matter, let us review the three roles this statement, 'I am Z.V.', may play. For you, the listener, it may mean either of two things. First, in an introduction it merely adds one feature, namely that I am called Z.V., to your emerging image of me. In understanding and accepting what I say, you simply learn a contingent fact about me. In this role that statement is not a statement of identity: its logical form is not $a=b$, but simply Fa.

Second, it can function as a means of identification, connecting two representations you have of me. As we recall, this happens, for instance, when you already know of me by name, and are confronted with me in the flesh without knowing that I am that man. In this case, indeed, that statement is understood as a statement of identity: $a=b$.

Finally, for me, it may carry the burden of placing me in the world. In this role, it attributes the state of being Z.V., i.e. being "there" in the universe, to me. Thus, again, its form is not to be represented by $a=b$. Should it be then by Fa? Not quite; for here the I does not pick out an object, a thing, in the field of experience; it marks the ultimate subject, the transcendental self. For the fun of it, let us write Fi, with the understanding that the i is not an ordinary referring expression: it is not a name of something which could be denoted by some other name too.

In view of these considerations the worrying aspect of transference may be allayed. I am, actually, in the state of being Z.V.; but in imagining, say, being R.R., I fancy being in another state, which actually is not the case.

3. Is there anything wrong with this view? Things, in general, are in a certain state at any given moment, but, as time goes by, their state may change: the well man becomes ill, and the like. Moreover, for a given time too, they *could* be in a different state: my dirty hands could now be clean if I had washed them a minute ago.

All these things are possible and imaginable. I am healthy now, but I can imagine having the flu, etc. In this case my fancy alters my present state only slightly, for it is still being Z.V. that I imagine, albeit enduring the symptoms of the flu.

In imagining being someone else, however, I do something far more radical. In the very act of representing that other mind, nothing specific is left of being Z.V.—what has to remain is the general framework of human consciousness. But, as we remember, this feat is still not the limit of transference. In imagining being that cat, for instance, nothing will be left beyond the "conditions of all experience" or "unity of consciousness": an empty "I", the transcendental self.

This solution, on the face of it, is simplicity itself. Think of a TV screen showing Dan Rather reading the evening news. Now, I certainly can imagine Barbara Walters doing that on the same screen; or, again, the tube showing John Wayne riding into the sunset. Whatever it shows, however, has to conform to an a priori form of presentation: 19" across, 525 lines from side to side . . . Consider, then, the TV screen as the transcendental "I", actually occupied by one presentation (my present consciousness), but potentially open to any presentation preserving the "format" of the unity of consciousness (the mind of Hannibal, Reagan, or the cat). Concerning this format I will not say anything more. Practically, we know what it means; otherwise we could not even attempt to perform transference. Theoretically—what could I add to the work of Kant and his interpreters?

4. People will object, of course, to this idea of the "transcendental self made simple". Let us review some of the possible objections, starting from the easier ones.

'Your consciousness is spread out in time—and so is Ronald Reagan's. Accordingly, imagining being R.R. requires more than replacing one picture on the screen by another. For one thing, how do you know that what you imagine is not a possible stage of your own conscious life?'

I reply by invoking Kant's remark that the conscious life of a person is but a single phenomenon, albeit spread out in time.[1] My consciousness, as we explained in Chapter V, is the connected sequence of experiences matching the history of my bodily existence; and so is R.R.'s matching his. Thus, in imagining being he sitting in the Oval Office now, I fit an imagined mental state into a series determined by his personal history, reflected in his concurrent memories, associations, anticipations, and so forth. A snapshot of a game (a process in time) connotes the past and the future; a glimpse into a mind (a temporal manifold) has to do the same.

'But the picture-tube is a thing in the field of experience—but the "I" you describe is pure form.' I agree, and here is where our *similitudo incipit claudicare*. The transcendental "I" is not a thing, it has no content; it is a frame into which any content may fit, or, better, a "format" or a "schema" into which any content may be cast. As the Kantian schema of a triangle is not an object to be perceived but a "rule" to

[1] *Critique of Practical Reason*, p. 99.

be followed, so is the "schema of subjectivity", which, as I see it, is at least one aspect of the transcendental self.[2]

5. 'Your simile limps on another leg, too. The TV screen, whatever it displays, is viewed by *you*, who are outside the picture. But when you imagine, e.g. being Ronald Reagan, your act of imagining belongs to the mind of Z.V., which is but one of the pictures that transcendental "screen" can display. So, according to your view, it is one "picture", or part of one picture, which contemplates another.'

This is a harder objection, but not insurmountable. First, I have to grant that the act of imagination representing the mind of R.R., or whomever, belongs to my mind, i.e. Z.V.'s mind. And, in this sense, it is that mind which performs the transference. In another sense, however, in the transcendental sense, it is the contentless "I" which is the agent of this act, just as much as it is the subject of all the experiences that make up Z.V.'s mind. After all, as we explained in detail, this mind's being mine is a matter of access, and not of content. Now, whether I imagine a tree, a sea-battle, or being R.R., the representation evoked will appear in the temporal framework, and against the background, of this particular mind. Thus when you say that what Z.V. is doing now is imagining being R.R. in the Oval Office, this will be true if I evoke that subjective representation with the resources of my mind, Z.V.'s mind, i.e. the mind to which I have a privileged access, and—we may add now, to anticipate things—the content of which, to some extent at least, is at my free disposal.

To return to the picture analogy: as there are pictures within pictures (think of Vermeer), so there can be representations of other subjects, not merely of objects, within the unity of one's own consciousness. In seeing a picture within a picture, one shifts perspective from the encompassing picture to the encompassed; in performing transference, one shifts the focus of the "I" from the encompassing self to the encompassed. But the eye of sight, and the "I" of consciousness, remain the same.

Moreover—let us not forget—the person thus represented may be oneself: that body and, via "imaginary expectations", that mind. This is what happens, for instance, when I visualize *myself* walking on the moon in a cumbersome space-suit, and then imagine what it must be like to be in that condition. Or, simply, I can evoke the image of my present state, in body and in mind, as a feature of that "centreless"

[2] *Critique of Pure Reason*, A 141, B 180; KS 182-3.

world view projected in Chapter I. This is, in fact, how I have to represent what I am, and come to know who I am. Van Eyck could paint
himself painting Arnolfini in the mirror. I can represent my mind, or
another mind, in my mind with equal ease: it depends on which body
I pick to begin with.

What I cannot represent, however, is the subject of all these acts:
the "I" that projects the pictures and views the show, that creates the
representations of all things, including conscious beings in body and in
mind, and of myself in the same way. The eye cannot see the eye,
except in an image—and the "I" cannot perceive the "I", except as
it appears as a body among other bodies in the world of experience,
and as a mind, among other minds, evoked in imagination by applying
the "schema of subjectivity" to that body. The ultimate subject of all
representations defies representation. Being aware of myself is being
aware of the tie that connects me to that one person in the world.[3]

6. Finally the toughest challenge. 'This is all very fine, if you restrict
your attention to your own case. But, as you repeatedly argued, you do
not enjoy any privileged position among the conscious beings in the
world. Here I am, as good a subject as you. Am I entitled, then, to my
own little transcendental self, distinct from yours, which has the same
kind of access to my mind as yours does to yours?'

No, you are not, I reply, but nor am I. I have a mind, but I do not
"have" a transcendental self: the ultimate subject cannot be had. It is
like the *materia prima*, not really one and certainly not many, which
cannot be "received" (but remember St. Thomas's verdict on David
de Dinant, which applies here too).[4] Or Averroës's active intellect—
common to all men. How, in the first place, could there be many *contentless* beings, not located in space and time either? How would they
differ from one another? 'By the relations they bear to this and that
individual mind', you suggest.[5] If so, I reply, then "my" transcendental
self would be essentially tied to me, thus, once more, transference
would be impossible: I could not imagine being Ronald Reagan,
because I could not *be* in the state of being he. But I can: *ergo* . . .

[3] I would like to think that these views have an affinity not only to Kant's
doctrine, but also to Wittgenstein's remarks about the self, both in the *Tractatus*
(nos. 5. 6 ff.) and in the *Investigations* (I, 404–11).

[4] 'Who most absurdly thought that God was primary matter' (*Summa Theologica*, I. 3. 8).

[5] Somewhat in the way Scholastic doctrine explains the individuality of
separated souls by their "transcendental" relation to the bodies they left behind.

'You mean to say, then, that you *could* be R.R., Napoleon, or I?'
Yes, I answer, I could have been born as any of these personages. This
follows from three assumptions we established before:

(a) whatever is imaginable is possible (subject to the qualifications
added in Chapter II);

(b) being, say, Napoleon is a phenomenon extended in time (as
explained a few pages back);

(c) the essential feature of being that man, Napoleon, is his "insertion into history" (see Chapters II and IV).

Hence, since I can imagine being Napoleon, it follows that I could
have been born as Napoleon . . . or R.R., or you. By the same token,
I could have been born in the Middle Ages, as a Chinaman, or even
perhaps as a pig or a bat. All these things are impossible for Z.V., but
possible for *me*.[6]

If, therefore, I had been born as Napoleon, then I would be
Napoleon; i.e., the very same "I", which actually recognizes himself
in Z.V., would recognize himself in Napoleon. To use the familiar
terminology: the very same "I" would be in another state. The same
thing holds in regard to your state; consequently you do not have
another transcendental self.

A word of caution is in order here. As we noted above, the 'I' in
the statement 'I am Z.V.' (taken in the sense in which it locates me in
the world) must not be understood as a name that could be replaced
by another name or referring expression. It does not denote a thing
(physical or mental) in the world to which a name could be tied, or of
which a description could be true. What it marks (does not "denote") is
the ultimate subject of all representations of which no representation
can be formed. Accordingly, this 'I' cannot enter into non-trivial
identity statements, since the function of such a statement is to
connect two representations of the same thing. My claims, therefore,
that it is the *same* "I" that underlies transference, and the *same* "I"
that could be in another state, have to be understood entirely *via nega-
tiva*: not distinct, and not different. Thus, the unity of this "I" is not
like the unity of material things (one of the many in the same kind),
not even like the "essential" unity of abstract forms or numbers;[7] for
all these things can be named and identified in many ways. Thus we
are driven back to the desperate analogy of the "prime matter": *neque*

---

[6] See my 'A Note to the Paralogisms'.
[7] *Summa Theologica*, I. 11, 3.

quid, neque quale, neque quantum . . . , yet nothing either. One more instance of the great strain under which our concepts labour in these matters.

7. As we mentioned above, there are all sorts of objects which can be *now* in this state, *then* in that. Substances, as Aristotle noticed, can change in time. This account of alternative states, however, cannot apply to the transcendental self. It is not in the world, not in time, and in general not subject to the categories governing the manifold of experience.

Indeed, in discussing transference, we do not envisage the "I" donning successive "incarnations", as it were: transference has nothing to do with transmigration. I could be someone else in a timeless sense: Napoleon in the eighteenth century, or R.R. now. The question is not what, I actually was or will be, but what, or who, I potentially could be.

Thus the analogy is not the dirty hand that was clean an hour ago, but the dirty hand that could be clean now if it had been washed a minute ago. In this case, of course, considerations of time enter the picture. But, even with ordinary substances, this is not necessarily so: this red flower could be blue if the plant had been treated with some chemical.

If so, then there is nothing incomprehensible about the possibility of my having been born as Napoleon instead of Z.V. Of course, the alternative colours of that flower put it into different possible worlds, but my being Z.V. or Napoleon need not change the world. Accordingly, the possibility of my being somebody else escapes the possible world-treatment. If you like names, it is not a natural, but a "transcendental" possibility, solely based on imaginability. In a similar way, now being 1815 is a transcendental possibility, since I can imagine being Napoleon at the battle of Waterloo. As I can alight in fancy on another body and mind in the world, claiming them as mine without disturbing anything, so can I alight on another moment, making it a "now" without changing an iota of history.

8. 'Thank you kindly for making me into a transcendental possibility,' you protest indignantly. 'What you say is this: the one and only transcendental self actually happened to "alight" on you—it might have descended upon me, but *de facto* it did not. So I have to be satisfied with the crumbs of possibility falling down from your table . . . Am I, as a person, but a projection of your benevolent imagination? And this after all that prattle about "no privileged status"!'

Z.V. has no privileged status, I reply; my being Z.V. does not bestow any favours on Z.V., does not add anything to the nature of this man. But I *am* this person, and not you, and this means that I am connected, by the double links of access and disposal, to this individual. I recognize at the same time, however, that this is but a (transcendentally) contingent tie: that is to say, that I could be another conscious being.

In order to show that this unique link does not detract anything from your, and other people's, reality, I shall invoke once more the "I" 's analogy to the "now". This morning's sunshine is no less real than the battle of Waterloo. Yet the sunshine is now, and that battle lies in the past. But to Napoleon and Wellington it occurred as now on that fatal day. Moreover, in evoking that engagement in my imagination I have to represent it as occurring now, i.e. as something open to the senses; for, remember, what I imagine is seeing, hearing, and feeling things. And nothing can be seen, heard, etc., "from the past", unless it is rendered present by the effort of fantasy.

Then I ask: how many "now" 's are there? If you say, as many as there are moments of history, you are trivially right, but basically wrong. Indeed, any moment of time is now at that moment. But this answer falls short of doing justice to the actual now: the unique moment of our present experience, at which the privileged access to our mental states terminates and free disposal begins. And, of course, in representing the past as now (say, in imagining being Napoleon on the day of Waterloo), I have to fancy being in that state with respect to access and disposal; for, after all, he was a man perceiving and acting on the field.

Long ago we reflected on the "indexicality" of the self; and obviously the "now" is equally indexical. But this realization cannot provide the ultimate answer to the problems of self and now, simply because it does not single out the actual self and the actual now. To say that every moment is a now, and that every person is a self, does not answer the question what time it is, and who I am.

Thus, the day of Waterloo is as real as today, and I would represent it falsely if I fancied it otherwise. And you, and Napoleon, are as real as Z.V., and I would be at fault if I did not represent you or him as such. But I am Z.V., and now it is 12-8-10-81. We explained above that the former of these assertions is not to be written as $i = Z.V.$, but rather as Fi, where the F means something like 'is in the state of being Z.V'. Similarly, the latter assertion's form is not $n = 12\text{-}8\text{-}10\text{-}81$, but rather Gn, where G means something like 'is at 12-8-10-81'. As the "now" is not identical with this moment, the transcendental "I" is not identical with Z.V. I am Z.V., in the sense just explained, but in no sense am I the transcendental self, let alone "have" it. So, to allay your fears, I do not appropriate that self. If anything, the transcendental "I" "has" me, as it "has" you and Napoleon. But since I am *this* man, it is my mind that appears actual to me, and yours only projected. The fact, however, that I *can* project it as another "self" demonstrates the transcendental aspect of my consciousness: I *could* be somebody else.

The transcendental "I" is not Z.V., not you, and not Napoleon. Yet I become conscious of myself as Z.V., you as you, and Napoleon as Napoleon. That is to say, the transcendental "I" can appear as various "empirical" selves. 'I am Z.V.', we said, means 'I am in the state of being Z.V.' Now we can put it in another way: I appear to myself as being Z.V. But it is a contingent appearance.

'But'—a last objection—'how can that same self be in all these states at the same time?'

It is not 'at the same time'. Time, a feature of the empirical world, has no meaning for the transcendental "I". It "touches" the world, as we suggested above, at the various "anchors of subjectivity", organisms scattered in space and time. It is thus related to the world in many ways, creating the various perspectives in which the mental life of conscious individuals consists. To borrow Leibniz's words: I am a living mirror of the universe; this body reflecting the light of the transcendental self in its own unique way in my mind.

B. COGITO

9. At the beginning of this chapter I attributed, no doubt correctly, the idea of a transcendental self to Kant. Yet it can be argued that its origins lie in Descartes's *Cogito*-argument.

I do not wish to add anything new to the exegesis of the passages involved.[8] I shall assume, however, that in the most "solemn" expression of the argument, in *Meditation Two*, Descartes said exactly what he meant. And what he said is this: 'the statement "I am, I exist" is necessarily true every time it is uttered by me or conceived in my mind.'[9]

---

[8] I did try such an exegesis in *Res Cogitans*, Chapter VII.
[9] '. . . Hoc pronuntiatum, *Ego sum, ego existo*, quoties a me profertur, vel mente concipitur, necessario esse verum' (AT VII, 25; Cress 17).

In order to avoid difficulties that might arise out of switching personal pronouns I shall proceed as if I, Z.V., had written those lines.
With this understanding the passage claims that whenever I think that
I exist, it follows that it is necessarily true that I exist. What does it
mean, that this is necessarily true? It is quite clear that for Descartes
it means that its contradictory, namely that I do not exist, is inconceivable.[10]

From several related passages in *Meditation Two* and elsewhere, it
appears that the same move can be made starting out from any thought
I might entertain: when I think that this is a piece of wax, or that I am
breathing now, etc., it cannot be the case that I do not exist.[11] Accordingly, if I begin with the very thought of my own existence, I immediately see that it *cannot* be false, i.e. that its contradictory, namely
that I do not exist, is inconceivable.

But, surely, I am no God, no necessary being. I, Z.V., might never
have come into existence, or, even if I did, I might have expired long
ago. If my father had died in World War I, I would not have been
born, and if I had succumbed to diphtheria at the age of seven, I would
not be around to think about these matters. My non-existence now, in
other words, is perfectly conceivable.

And, of course, we must credit Descartes, too, with such a simple
insight. Accordingly, some people interpret him as saying, not that
whenever he thinks he necessarily exists, but simply that it is necessarily
true that, whenever he thinks, he exists.[12] Switching back to the first
person again, this difference can be made clear as follows:

(1) (t) (I think . . . at t → □ I exist at t)
(2) (t) □ (I think . . . at t → I exist at t)

(1) gives our original interpretation, and (2) the one just mentioned.
(2) may be generalized:

(3) (x) (t) □ (x thinks . . . at t → x exists at t)

This, in turn, is but an application of a still more general maxim, to
wit:

(4) (x) (t) □ (x acts at t → x exists at t)

[10] This is obvious from his version of the Ontological Argument. He says, for
instance, in *Meditation Five*: 'from the fact that I cannot think of God except as
existing, it follows that existence is inseparable from God' (Cress 42).

[11] *Meditation Two* (Cress 22), *Letter* (to xxx), March 1638 (AT II, 37).

[12] e.g. Frankfurt in *Demons, etc.*, pp. 105–6.

which means that action entails existence (*one* sense of the medieval principle *agere sequitur esse*).

What distinguishes thinking for Descartes' purposes is its epistemic status: one can be mistaken about sitting before the fireplace, but not about thinking that one sits before the fireplace, or thinking that one exists. Thus even this version is sufficient to exorcize the demon.

Thus interpreted, the *Cogito* does not generate the paradox of the inconceivability of my current non-existence. Since, in fact, I think that I exist, it necessarily follows that I exist; but, of course, if I did not exist now, I would not be thinking anything. And this seems to be a perfectly conceivable state of affairs.

To see this, consider the parallel argument involving saying something and talking, instead of thinking and existing.[13] In its general form it comes out as

(t) $\square$ (I say . . . at t → I am talking at t)

And self-applied:

(t) $\square$ (I say 'I am talking' at t → I am talking at t).

I can conclude, therefore (sloppily, I think, as I shall presently argue), that 'the statement "I am talking" is necessarily true every time it is uttered by me'. This does not mean, however, that it is inconceivable that I might not be talking at this time. I am not that loquacious: I could have remained silent.

One more example showing the difference just explained. It is necessarily true that whenever I am eating I am eating. But, even if I am actually eating, I do not do it necessarily; I might have postponed my meal.

10. Does (2) above indeed represent the correct interpretation of the *Cogito*? Is, furthermore, my current non-existence a conceivable state of affairs? I think that the answer to either of these questions is in the negative.

As I mentioned a while ago, it is reasonable to assume that Descartes, in giving the *Cogito*-argument in *Meditation Two, loquitur formaliter*. Granted, those lines can be read in the sense of (2), but it is not the only reading, and certainly not the most obvious one. So, we are entitled to ask, if what he meant was only the conditional necessity of (2), why did not he say so? He certainly could have

[13] I called this the Dico-argument in *Res Cogitans* (p. 199).

(e.g. '. . . necesse esse hoc pronuntiatum, . . . quoties a me . . . concipitur, esse verum').

A fortiori, why does he continue 'But I do not yet understand well enough who I am—I, who now necessarily exist (. . . qui jam necessario sum)'?[14] I do not see how this statement can be understood in the sense of (2).

Nevertheless, I do not consider the textual evidence decisive, for after all he might have confused the two kinds of necessity.[15] There is, however, a more compelling argument against taking the *Cogito* in the sense of (2). If that interpretation were correct, then it would not matter how Descartes refers to himself in establishing his existence, since (2) is but an instance of (3). Instead of *I*, he might have used *René Descartes*, his serial number (he had been a soldier), or an identifying description, without any harm to the validity of the move.[16]

But, of course, at that stage in the *Meditations* he does not yet know anything about himself: not his name, not his nature, nor any other particular. If so, then the fact that Mr. Descartes is a contingent entity, i.e. a thing the non-existence of which is conceivable, is irrelevant to the sense of the *Cogito*.

Thus he is left with "I", about which he knows nothing. 'According to the laws of true Logic, the question "*does a thing exist*?" must never be asked unless we already understand *what the thing is*.'[17] Yet he sees that that "I", about which he knows nothing, must exist. What, then, is this "I"? A thinking thing, he says later on: 'precisely only a thing that thinks'.[18] A "thing" in other words, which has no content, but which is by necessity the subject of all thoughts, since its existence follows from any thought . . .

The fact that Descartes himself came to think that the "I" of the *Cogito* is identical with Mr. Descartes's soul should not matter. In this, as Kant has shown, he was mistaken. The important thing is what the *Cogito can* prove, not what Descartes thought it can.

11. What does it mean to say that I might not exist now? Obviously that this man, Z.V. (born to those parents, etc.), might not exist

[14] AT VII, 25; Cress 17.
[15] Indeed the French text of the last quotation says 'moy qui suis certain que je suis' (AT IX, I. 19).
[16] Think of Hintikka's remarks about the "existential inconsistency" of de Gaulle's uttering 'de Gaulle does not exist' in '*Cogito, Ergo Sum* . . .', pp. 14 ff.
[17] *Reply I* (AT VII, 108; HR II, 13).   [18] *Meditation Two* (Cress 19).

now; in other words, that one can conceive of the world and history without this particular person altogether, or in such a way that he dies before this date; or again, if you like to put it that way, that there are possible worlds not containing Z.V., or containing him for a shorter period than my present age. All these possibilities are perfectly conceivable, and I can conceive of them at this moment. But, of course, to conceive of these situations, or *any situation whatsoever*, I must exist. I, the subject of all these representations, remain invariant: I can remove in thought Descartes, Napoleon, Z.V., the earth, the moon, or any of the stars, but I cannot remove myself. *My* non-existence, unlike that of Z.V., is inconceivable. In this sense 'I exist' is necessarily true whenever and whatever I think, and the fate of Z.V. is neither here nor there.

What Descartes's argument (even if not Descartes . . .) proves is not the existence of any "thing" (body, soul, substance, or property) in the world, but the "existence" of an empty and contentless "I", which however is the a priori and necessary form and subject of all possible representations. In other words, the "existence" of a transcendental self.[19]

'But what if I remove in thought all rational, nay, all sensitive beings from the world, for example by imagining the process of evolution not getting beyond the trees? Surely, there are possible worlds like that, and I can conceive of them. Yet in those worlds there would be no representations, thus no need for a transcendental self.' My answer is this: you who envisage such worlds would exist anyway, but you could not find yourself in any of the creatures of *those* worlds. As the transcendental self does not "belong" to you or me, it does not "belong" to any conceivable world either. By showing that there might be such "soulless" worlds, you do not show that the transcendental self might not exist; all you show is that in such worlds it would not find a home.

Of course, the transcendental self does not operate by itself, *in vacuo*, but as anchored in you or me. For this reason the idea of a possible world not containing rational creatures is mere speculation. I exist, by Descartes's argument, since I perceive and think and act in *some* subject in the world, which *happens to be* this mind and this

---

[19] The scare-quotes around 'existence' in these lines mark my agreement with Kant that existence, strictly speaking, is a category applicable to things in the manifold of experience. Similarly the aspect of time belongs to the representation and not to the "I". Descartes makes his first *faux pas* in asking 'But for how long?' (*Cress* 18).

body. To use Kant's terminology: the transcendental unity of apperception does not determine *my* perspective; it is the rule for all possible perspectives.

C. AGENCY

12. Towards the end of Chapter V we developed a notion of free agency, which combined causal determinism in our representation of the objective world, with the possibility of free choice in regard to certain series of events originating in one's own bodily movements. The price we had to pay for this solution consisted in the admission that one cannot have, at any given moment of time, a complete concurrent representation of the objective world. We remarked, however, that such incompleteness is an essential prerequisite anyway for our ability to find ourselves in the universe: one's being "there" (with an empirical self and a "now") is a function of privileged access, and this, in turn, is incompatible with an omniscient mind. Laplace's demon, if he existed, would be a disembodied and timeless being.

The world, therefore, for each of us, and for any moment of our conscious lives, remains determinable, to some extent at least, by free actions. Nevertheless, the processes resulting from such acts will appear as causally linked to the rest of the universe. The exercise of free will does not create gaps in the causal texture of the world; it consists in realizing one unbroken causal sequence rather than some others. Remember, in raising my arm I actualize a causal chain leading up to and following from the physical event of my arm's going up. The "retroactive" element, i.e. the antecedent physical conditions causing my arms to go up, is as much dependent upon my choice as the sequel of that motion (touching the lamp, etc.). It is exactly for this reason that at the moment of choice my representation of the world cannot be complete (e.g. including the micro-state of my organism).[20]

This retroactive feature of the exercise of free will may take some effort to accept. It seems like an instance of "backward causality". As I said before, however, the exercise of the will is not an instance of causality at all, since it does not operate on the same level as natural causes; it does not compete or interfere with such causes. Nevertheless,

---

[20] Thus I go beyond Chisholm's claim (stated in 'Freedom and Action') that the agent causes the brain-event which causes the bodily motions necessary for his action. The agent, I say, selects the whole causal chain in which that brain-event is but a link.

to a limited extent, it determines what is to happen in the world. In order to facilitate the comprehension of such non-causal determination of events, I shall give two analogies, one quite familiar to all of us, the other to theologians at least.

Think of a writer seeking to "eliminate" one of his characters in the novel he is composing. For reasons of his own he prefers a blameless way, death as a result of an accident, or "act of God". Shall it be an earthquake, storm, fire, or what? Well, he will choose one of these possibilities, and build it into his story. In doing so, however, he cannot just create, say, fire *ex nihilo*: he has to sketch, or at least allow for, the antecedents (e.g. how the house caught fire), and weave the whole sequence into the fabric of his story. Did *he*, the writer, cause the fire? Not at all, the heater's explosion caused it. Yet it was up to him whether there be a fire at all. His determination, moreover, that there be a fire at some time in the story, remains outside the temporal framework of the novel; one can write a story taking place in the nineteenth century now.

The other analogy is taken from the traditional doctrine of God's "causality" with respect to the processes in the world. God, except in miracles, does not interfere with the operation of mundance causes, yet they all conform to his design. His influence is not ordinary causality, but *concursus*: God *fortiter et suaviter* makes the causes cause according to their nature. And, once more, although his "works" are in time, his activity is not.

In raising my arm on set purpose, I do not cause my arm to go up: it goes up becomes some muscles contracted, and this because some neurons fired, and this because . . . etc. But I am the one who writes this little incident into my life's book; I am the one who makes the causes cause in service of my designs. And although the motions thus produced are in time, the exercise of my freedom in selecting this particular sequence of events cannot be placed in time, since then it would be itself conditioned by the antecedent processes of nature. To put it concisely: temporal relations hold between the phases of the process I bring about in the world, but not between them and my act of bringing them about.[21] The "now", as we pointed out in the previous

---

[21] This is the reason, by the way, for the awkwardness of such questions as 'When, exactly, did Sirhan kill Kennedy?' (when he fired the gun?, when the victim died? . . .), or 'When, exactly, did Jane roast the chicken?' (when she set the timer on the oven? . . .). The events which form the causal chain are easily datable; the doing by the agent is not.

chapter, is not a relation of simultaneity between two events, but a window of access, for awareness and action, between the changing world and me. And this "me", the abiding and empty form of consciousness, cannot change; thus, is not in time.

13. But, of course, the agency of the transcendental self does not operate *in vacuo*: as I recognize myself in this person, so my agency appears in actions performed in time. For although my acts are not caused by anything in the world, they are done for reasons perceived in the temporal stream of my consciousness, and their subsequent execution is also registered there in the form of appropriate experiences. In doing something intentionally (say, switching on the light) I select a course of action in view of the knowledge, beliefs, needs, and desires I possess at a certain moment of my life, and then I experience the execution of that act, in the form of kinaesthetic, visual, and other perceptions, all neatly placed in the order of time.

The point is, however, that the very exercise of my "efficacy", the "act of will" which actualizes this sequence of events, does not appear at all in my experience; it is not an additional event that could be perceived as occurring between my thoughts and deliberations about the deed to be done, and the awareness of the act's being performed. "The moment of choice" we mentioned a while ago is not the instant of time at which some invisible muscle (the will or similar agency) gets exercised, but simply the moment of time at which deliberation leaves off, and action (if one is decided upon) begins. Of course, in the ordinary course of daily life we do things routinely, without conscious deliberation, yet many of the things we do in this way still qualify as intentional actions. In these activities there is no "moment of choice", no temptation to think that there must be a "push" by the will to bring us to a decision between the available alternatives.

14. But surely there must be a difference between merely perceiving what happens to my body, and being aware of the bodily actions I perform. There has to be a difference, say, between the awareness of a muscular spasm, and that of a voluntary flexing of a muscle. Now, since we just said that one cannot be aware of one's efficacy *ex principio*, it has to manifest itself *ex termino*, in other words, in the way we are aware of our bodily actions. Such a result will be in accordance with our prevous finding that the relation between the self and its manifestation in the world is a matter of access.

Suppose I raise my arm in order to switch on the lamp. It is getting dark, I don't see clearly the page, yet I want to go on writing. These are my reasons, if reasons are called for, for turning on the light. So I raise my arm, reach the lamp, and push the button. What does this mean? Is it enough to merely feel and see my arm going up, etc., to be able to say that I do these things? Certainly not; for it is possible to have the experience of my arm going up as a result of a spasm or the manipulation of a clever neurophysiologist on my brain. And this experience, even if it occurred after some thoughts about switching on the light, would not count as an experience of raising my arm. What is missing? It is not sufficient to say that the motion of my arm has to fit an intention to raise my arm, because I may even have formulated such an intention in my mind before the 'spasm' occurred.

Ask yourself, how do you know that your arm is going up? In the "spasm" case the answer is simple: you can "feel" (kinaesthetic, muscular sensations), or even see, the arm going up. But what if you raise you arm intentionally? In this case you do not have to wait, as it were, for the testimony of the senses to arrive to realize what is going on. You know what *you* are doing directly, under a description, and the incoming data of the senses concerning the state of your body merely fit into the schema evoked by that description. Think of actions of the following type: tying a necktie, dancing a waltz, signing your name, all done in pitch dark. Then imagine the same motions being enacted as a result of spasms or brain stimulation. Would you recognize, from the bare sensations, what they amount to? What does it "feel" like silently articulating, or writing down blindfolded, the word *tintinnabulation*? I would not know, yet I can do these things, and would know what I am doing in going through the motions.

The situation is quite different, however, for a witness observing you. He indeed can only conclude what you are doing on the basis of the external circumstances and the motions of your limbs: he has to discover the pattern of action into which those movements might fit. You, the agent, are aware of the pattern to begin with, and can await the report of the senses confirming execution.

But what if the report of the senses falls short of your expectations, e.g. you wrote down that word with a letter missing? Even then, you still know what you *tried* to do.

Thus we encounter once more a special access to one's condition in the world: as subjective experience represents a privileged access to some of one's bodily states, so does the awareness of what one is doing represent a similar access to what one brings about in the world as an agent. But whereas the former access is sensory, the second is conceptual: one is directly aware of what one is doing, or trying to do, under a description.

And it is this fact that enables us to relate our actions to the intentions we might have formed in view of our reasons, aims, and the like. For as these things are apprehended on the conceptual level, so their fulfilment, the action performed, must be apprehended conceptually, i.e. performed under a description. This tie between reasons, intentions, and execution may be explicit and conscious in fully deliberated actions, or implicit and subconscious in routine activity. We do not deliberate while spooning up the soup from our plate; yet we know what we are doing—without waiting for, and interpreting, the delivery of the senses.

What a person is doing is an action, and is free, not because it is done for reasons, follows deliberation, and conforms to an intention, but the other way around: one can have reasons, one can deliberate, and form intentions, because free actions appear to the agent not merely in the form of sensory awareness of bodily motions, but as something *he* is doing under a description, i.e. something directly apprehended in conceptual terms.

15. There is a widespread view in the Empiricist tradition of Hume and Mill, which tries to reconcile freedom of action with the demands of causality, often called "soft determinism". According to this view, freedom is not curtailed if what the agent does is "caused" by his desires, beliefs, intentions, choices, and so forth. Since these factors belong to the agent's own consciousness, their causality with respect to the action performed appears to be a case of self-determination.

Such a view presupposes a peculiar picture of the human mind. The first element in this picture is Hume's familiar "bundle-theory" of the self. A mind is nothing but a sum of perceptions and ideas, among which rank the desires, beliefs, etc. mentioned above. The other element is a "vector-space" conception of the interaction between these constituents. Desires and wants combine with beliefs into reasons for action in many ways, and, in case of conflict, the stronger combination (of reasons, or reasons aided by untamed passions) carries the day. Thus the forthcoming action is causally determined, but determined by the subject himself, i.e. by factors that make up that subject.

The first trouble with this view is the following. How is it possible that reasons, desires, and the like, which are elements of a consciousness, can cause overt actions, which involve bodily movements? If the theory is understood dualistically, then it leads into the blind alley of Cartesian interaction between mind and body. If, on the other hand, it is combined with a materialistic position, then the self-determination of the agent will amount to nothing more than the "freedom" of a turnspit, clock, or computer.

In either case, the "paramechanical" model of reasons as causes flies in the face of our intuitions about freedom and responsibility which it was designed to preserve. If this view were correct, then the criminal could plead in the dock as follows: 'I indeed killed the grocer, Your Honour, but given my desire for money, my knowledge of his weakness, and my low opinion of police efficiency, I could not have done otherwise. I had no good reasons to spare him except moral reasons, and these happen to be somewhat undernourished in my make-up . . .'

By and large, people indeed act rationally. And this fact accounts for the "predictability" of other persons' conduct which Hume and his followers mention in support of their position. Unfortunately, however, people can be selective about the very reasons they bring to bear upon their choices. So there is no guarantee that the objectively "strongest" reason will win out. And, in the subjective domain, the "strength" of a reason will be the function of the agent's preference. The criminal chose to follow his overwhelming greed rather than the precepts of law or the dictates of the moral imperative. Yet he, and any other person, is capable of resisting his dominant inclinations, and even of improving himself, i.e. to alter the "bundle" of his present mental make-up; the very fact that one is capable of "not liking", or "being digusted with", oneself shows that the Humean self provides but the stage and the props for the actor's performance, who, in service of a higher law, *ought* to do his best with the material at his disposal. The Kantian "good will" is not a motive on par with the rest; it is no part of the "bundle".

16. Even aside of these troubles, however, the whole idea of agents (or their mental states) entering the causal network of the world, i.e. being on par with real causes, is based on a confusion between actions and events. In the following discussion I shall try to show, on the basis of common sense enshrined in language, that whereas events are the things that are typically caused, actions are *done* by agents, and not caused by anything.

'But is it not the case that overt actions at least are events? Consider, for instance, the breaking of a window. This is clearly an event, which takes place at a certain time, and which, accordingly, has to be caused by something or other. Yet, at the same time, the breaking of that window may be an action too: something that can be *done*, say, by children throwing stones. Their doing, therefore, must amount to causing an event.'

This objection overlooks the fact that such phrases as *the breaking of the window* are ambiguous between the intransitive and the transitive reading of the verbs. That phrase may come from *the window breaks* or (*somebody* or *something*) *breaks the window*. Now my claim is this: such expressions denote events with the intransitive reading, but actions with the transitive one. Accordingly, what they denote are things caused in the first instance, but things *done*, and not caused, in the second.

This can be made quite clear in the few cases in which the transitive forms are morphologically marked in the verb root: think of *rise-raise*, *fall-fell*, *lie-lay*, etc. For it is obvious that whereas the falling of the tree, and the rising of the flag, require causes, the felling of the tree and the raising of the flag do not: these things are done and not caused. It is nonsense to say that the *felling* of the tree was caused by Joe, or the wind, or that the *raising* of my arm was caused by me, my reasons, muscles, or what have you. What is true is that the *falling* of the tree was caused by the wind, and the *rising* of my arm by the contraction of some muscles. And these things in turn, to wit, the falling and the rising, cannot be done by anybody.

But is this "doing" not something like causation? At the first blush it seems that it is. When we say, for instance, that the wind felled the tree, we mean that the fall of the tree was caused by the wind. In a similar way, one might argue, the claim that I raised my arm must mean that the rising of my arm was caused by me. Again, the transitive occurrences of these verbs are called 'causative' by linguists, conforming to the intuition that agency is a form of causation.

Let us cast a closer look at the comparison between the "agency" of the wind, and other natural events, and the agency of a person. Indeed we can say that the wind felled the tree, or that the explosion broke the window, as well as we can say that Joe felled the tree, broke the window, or, for that matter, raised his arm. But there the similarity ends.

Consider the sentence:

(1) The explosion broke the window

and the corresponding versions explicitly using the word *cause*:

(2) The explosion caused the window to break
(3) The breaking of the window was caused by the explosion
(4) The explosion was the cause of the breaking of the window

All these sentences are perfectly acceptable, and so are the analogous sentences that could be formed about the wind and the tree, and the like.

But now take

(5) Joe broke the window

versus

(6) Joe caused the window to break
(7) ?The breaking of the window was caused by Joe
(8) *Joe was the cause of the breaking of the window

(6) is acceptable, provided that Joe achieved the result in a roundabout way (e.g. by belting out a high C). Not, however, if he just smashed his fist into the pane.[22] (7) is hardly comprehensible, and (8) fails altogether.

(6), as we just said, is saved by the possibility of doing things in an indirect way, i.e. *by* doing something else. Therefore not even this pattern is available for so-called "basic" actions, e.g. simply raising one's arm, or closing one's eye. Just try: 'Jim caused his eye to close—by doing what, one wonders.

Thus we see that whereas the "doings" of the wind and explosion can easily be described by fully causal statements, the "doings" of persons cannot. On the other hand, although we might say that natural events and forces "do" certain things, this is but an anthropomorphic metaphor, which breaks down under stress; questions like 'And what did the wind do next?' or 'And how did the explosion do it?' are very peculiar to say the least.

People (and animals to some extent) do things; events, forces, and the like, cause things. Reasons (or moods, beliefs, intentions, etc.) can do neither.

Yet we say things like 'His anger made him do it' (smash the pane), or even 'His belief that the air in the room was getting foul caused him

[22] Professor J. R. Ross has explained this point to me in a conversation. In the present discussion I am also using some of his results from his paper 'Act'.

to break the window.' Is this situation not analogous to 'The explosion caused the window to break'?

No, it is not. Once more, *break*, in . . . *caused him to break the window* is transitive, but *break* in *caused the window to break* is intransitive. Accordingly, the former "breaking" is an action, which is done by Joe, but the latter "breaking" is an event caused by the explosion.

'But then,' you insist, 'since his belief caused him to do what he did, his belief caused the action, even if not the event.'

I am willing to grant, I reply, that we use the verb *cause*, in a very restricted way, in this sense. But, once more, this employment of *cause* is a far cry from the way we use that word in stating causal connections between events in the world. To see this, consider these two sentences:

(9) His belief . . . caused him to break the window
(10) The lady caused the butler to open the door

(10) most likely means that the lady asked or ordered the butler to open the door. It does not imply at all that she *compelled* (say, by dire threats) or *forced* (physically) the man. Thus the butler could have refused to comply, notwithstanding the fact that the lady had given him a *reason* to do as bid.

In an exactly similar way, Joe's belief about the air may have provided him with a good reason to break the window. But he was by no means forced or compelled to do so; he could have done otherwise: break down the door, or put up with the smell. Unless, of course, he panicked, and acted compulsively.

Reasons, then, do not necessitate the outcome, but causes do. When we say, for instance, that the explosion has caused the breaking of the window we mean that *in that concrete situation* (think of all other "boundary conditions", or "causes" we do not care to mention, e.g. air-pressure, thickness of glass, etc.), the window could not but break given the explosion. Joe and the butler, however, could have done otherwise in the very same situations, notwithstanding Joe's belief, and the lady's request. Thus the verb *cause* has different implications in the two contexts. In a "natural" context *cause* connotes nomological necessity; in an "intentional" context it merely means something like (successfully) prompting.

Grammar follows suit: fully causal constructions are once more barred in the "intentional" cases. Compare

The breaking of the window was caused by the explosion

with

> *The butler's opening (of) the door was caused by the lady
> *Joe's breaking (of) the window was caused by his belief . . .

The use of the verb *cause* does not indicate a unitary concept; it only shows a "family resemblance". One must not argue, therefore, that since agents may be said to cause things, they must enter the causal chain of nature; and one must not argue that, since reasons can be said to cause agents to do things, they must determine the outcome. To do so would be similar to insisting that knowing how to swim must be the result of having learned certain facts.

We often act, finally, for no reason at all: think of whistling, stretching, or pacing the room. We know what we are doing, are not surprised by it, and could do otherwise. Yet, typically, we have no reasons to do these things. The idea that even in such cases the agent must have reasons, nay, jointly "compelling" reasons, for what he does is based on the prejudice of viewing actions as events, and reasons as causes.

17. Actions are done, we said, but events are caused. Yet overt actions at least "contain" events. It is time to clear up this connection.

Remember the example of raising one's arm. The event involved is the rising of the arm. The same relation holds with respect to all "basic" actions, whether or not the verb used is marked (or changed) in the transitive frame. Think of moving a finger (finger moves), bending a leg (leg bends), batting an eye (eye closes), and so forth: in general, moving one's body (one's body moves). The pattern holds for complex actions too: felling a tree (tree falls), breaking a window (window breaks), firing a gun (gun fires), killing a person (person dies), etc. The principle is this: an action-description consists of an event-description in a "causative" frame. To put it poetically: an action is an event with a handle.

Furthermore, since it is the action, and not the mere event, which is done, or performed, by the agent, in the full statement of what one does four elements are to be distinguished: the event, the action, the doing of the action, and the agent. Each of these can receive added modifications. Omitting the agent, I offer the following three sentences in which the adjuncts go with different elements:

Jim pulled the rope tight
Jim pulled the rope hard
Jim pulled the rope easily.

It is quite clear that *tight* is attached to the event description (rope gets tight); *hard* to the action description (hard pull); *easy* to the doing (easily done).[23]

An action, we just said, is an event with a handle. Events, however are members of causal chains. Thus, to continue the metaphor, to perform an action is to grab *a* handle (think of the description under which the action is performed) and pull the whole chain into reality. Accordingly what Joe did in breaking the window can be spelled out in Figure 3.

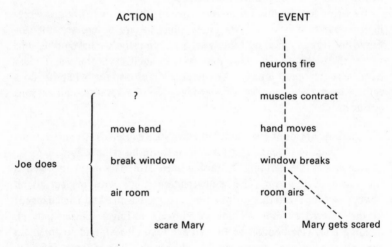

Figure 3

The schema in Figure 3 immediately accounts for the "accordion"-effect characteristic of real actions noted by Feinberg and Davidson. The latter writes: 'A man moves his finger, let us say intentionally, thus flicking the switch, causing the light to come on, the room to be illuminated, and the prowler to be alerted. This statement has the following

[23] Remember Austin's contrasting sentences:

Clumsily, he trod on the snail
He trod on the snail clumsily

(from 'A Plea for Excuses'). The first *clumsily* describes the manner of doing; the second, the quality of the action performed.

entailment: the man flicked the switch, turned on the light, illuminated the room, and alerted the prowler'.[24] Thus, whereas the efficacy of real causes does not jump links in the causal chain, the agent is related in the same way to the whole sequence. E.g. whereas it is not true that the movement of the man's finger scared the burglar, it is true that he moved his finger, scared the buglar, etc. This alone is sufficient to show that *he* is not a member of the causal chain. Agency introduces another dimension: to put it metaphorically, the agent's influence is "lateral" or "perpendicular" with respect to the line of causation.

The accordion-effect has its limits in both directions. The agent cannot be said to do things of which he *cannot* be aware "under a description". Thus, although the firing of his neurons does belong to the causal chain he actualized, Joe cannot be said to have fired his neurons. Similarly, but for a different reason, even if Mary (who had a heart-condition) is scared to death by the crash, Joe did not kill her (although, perhaps, caused her to die . . .), simply because he could not have foreseen this result.

One final remark. It is the agent that does things (performs actions), not his body. It is true, of course, that the body, and its parts, can "do" things in the weak sense mentioned above in connection with natural forces, and these doings too are often attributed to the person. When my mouth salivates I salivate, when my body shivers, I shiver. But, notice, I do not raise my arm because my arm goes up; on the contrary, when I do raise my arm, my arm goes up *because* I raise it. But it is nonsense to say that the palsied man's hand shakes because he shakes it.

Bodies, and their efficacy, belong to the space-time universe and its causal network. Agents, and their efficacy, do not, yet certain happenings in that very same world may be attributed to agency. This is possible, because we are able to represent, nay, we have to represent, certain organisms as bodies of *subjects* endowed with sensation, thought, and the power to act at will. As a result the "it" is viewed as a "he", and the event as an action. At the root lies our ability to perform transference, i.e. to lift the "I", in imagination, out of the contingent context of one's empirical self, and place it in another.

For this reason science, the study of the space-time universe, cannot find agency, as it cannot find pain, and in general, as it cannot find subjects, in its domain. Thus in these matters there is no way of appealing against the verdicts of intuition and common sense, made explicit by conceptual investigations, in a higher court of science. Those verdicts

[24] 'Agency', p. 53.

can be ignored (at the peril of losing one's own "place" in the cosmos), but cannot be reversed or overridden. In the matter of minds, as in the matter of morals, philosophy is on its own.

18. I sum up the discussion of agency in a more perspicuous, although inevitably somewhat misleading, form, in Figure 4.

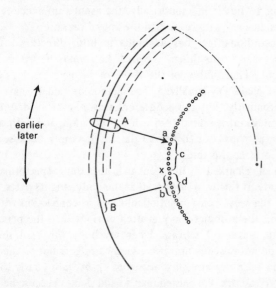

Figure 4

———— indicates an actual causal chain
– – – indicates a potential causal chain
———→ shows the deliveries of the senses corresponding to one's bodily state
ooooo indicates the stream of one's consciousness
–––→ represents the activity of the "I" in selecting one causal chain to become actual (this influence is not in time).

The sense of the diagram is this. At a I am aware of a state of my body, and of the world at point A. This awareness is compatible with many alternative causal chains going on in the world. c represents my conscious deliberation about a possible action (e.g. pushing the button to turn on the light, etc.). d represents my conceptual awareness of the resulting action (my pushing the button, etc.). b stands for the delivery of my senses corresponding to the execution of the act (muscular, visual sensations). B marks the objective state of affairs I bring about (arm rising, finger pushing, switch connecting, current flowing, etc.). B lies on the causal chain I activate by the "non-causal" agency of the transcendental self operating in me. The impact of this agency could be put anywhere on B's line, since it selects rather than modifies that line. x, finally, marks the "moment of choice" between deliberation and awareness of action. But, as we remember, the agency of the self is not in time: I pick that causal line *propter a et c*, but not *post a et c*.

19. The distinction between actions on the one hand, and mere bodily processes on the other, is not as sharp as we implied thus far. In order to remedy this over-simplification I shall sketch a few scenarios displaying the various possibilities in this matter.

There are, to begin with, actions full-blown, carefully deliberated and decided upon in advance of the deed. Think of such things as changing one's job, getting married, voting for a candidate, embarking on a journey, and so forth, not to speak of the examples, provided by mystery writers, of people planning and executing their crimes with full deliberation and "malice aforethought".

Then, there are actions routinely undertaken with no conscious awareness of reasons or motivation. When the smoker lights up a cigarette he does so, most of the time, unthinkingly, and would be hard put to explain why he did it at that moment. Nevertheless, this is not a compulsive act or mere reflex He knows what he is doing, and could postpone the enjoyment.

Examples of still more "attenuated" actions are the following: my nose itches, and I scratch it; I hear a noise and look in its direction. One would like to say that these are instances of reactions rather than actions, since the itch and the noise are like "causes" provoking them. Nevertheless, in most of such cases the agent could refrain from reacting: the guard in front of Buckingham Palace does not scratch and does not turn his head, come what may.

This is not the case with motions which are called reflexes. It is interesting to realize that perception and movement can be related in several ways within this domain of human and animal activity.

Consider, first, such reflexes as ducking one's head, and closing one's eyes, at the sudden approach of a fist or projectile. Here both the "stimulus" (the oncoming object) and the "response" (the ducking and the shutting) are perceived by the subject. One is tempted to say that here the "sight" (i.e. the subjective awareness) causes the response. Such an idea is less likely to arise in connection with the familiar knee-jerk reflex In this case we would be inclined to say that, although the subject feels the strike below the kneecap, it is not this feeling, but rather the mechanical impact upon the nerves, that causes the kick, which, incidentally, is also perceived. I would like to suggest that the temptation just mentioned should be resisted, and the ducking and eye-shutting reflexes should be explained in exactly the same way as the knee-jerk, i.e. by purely objective (neural) processes, which, however, occasion conscious awareness in the subject. Hence the lack of control in these cases: the above-mentioned guard will duck, and close his eyes, if you throw your camera in his face and will salivate at the smell of tasty food.

One difference, of course, between the ducking reflex and the knee-jerk is the following. Ducking, in those circumstances, is a "useful" move, but the knee-jerk is not. Accordingly we often duck, not as a reflex, but voluntarily to avoid some harm. So the impression is created that since the subjective experience of sight is involved in the "voluntary" ducking, the same experience "causes" the reflex ducking. This difference is connected with the fact that, whereas the causal chain leading to the ducking reflex involves some data-processing in the optic centre of the brain, which corresponds to visual experience, the knee-jerk is produced by a short cut, not involving the stimulation of the brain which occasions the feeling of being hit below the knee. Accordingly, one is more likely to report "I ducked" (rather than "I felt ducking") in the one case, but "I felt my leg kicking" (rather than "I kicked") in the other.

Then, consider such reflexes as the contraction of one's pupils at sudden bright light, the secretion of adrenalin at the perception of danger, and so forth. Here the subject is aware of the stimulus, but not of the response. The second example mentioned here, the adrenalin case, might raise the following difficulty. The perception of danger, unlike the impact of bright light, not only penetrates the subject's consciousness, but is likely to be the result of some "higher" mental capacities and processes: memory, evaluation, judgment, etc. Therefore, it looks again as if some bodily processes could be caused by subjective factors, in this case by conscious thought. I have to demur once more, however, and insist that, since for any subjective state there is a corresponding organic condition, this latter is the one that causes the reaction in the ordinary physical sense.

'But then,' you object, 'why don't you account for *all* actions in the same way? All the conscious (or subconscious) reasons, motives, intentions, etc., have their organic counterparts (i.e. neural states and pro-

processes); therefore the actions (i.e. the motions involved) can be determined by these factors without the mysterious non-causal intervention by an *ego ex machina*.'

My answer is that such "motions" as the secretion of adrenalin or the contraction of the pupils are not actions the person performs, but mere operations of his organs. Accordingly the person has no control over these processes: he cannot help their occurrence. But he does have control over his "intentional" actions; over processes, that is, which are perceived as his *doing* this or that. Of course, as I repeatedly claimed, even these operations can be viewed on a purely physiological level, and on that level they are indeed fully accountable for, in terms of the body's microstate. And for this reason the agent has to be able to determine not only the movements of his limbs, but the very state of his neural mechanism which causes them. This ability is *a fortiori* presupposed in actions not involving the motion of limbs and muscles, such as the control over one's thoughts. One can think of this or that at will, yet the thoughts involved are neurally based.

My answer comes down to this: I take freedom seriously. One ordinarily *cannot* keep the hands idle when falling on the face, even if promised a reward. But one *can* abstain from food even when starving (think of hunger-strikers), or go over the top on the battlefield in the teeth of dangers far greater than a bruised face.

I need not say anything about reflexes in which neither the stimulus nor the response penetrates consciousness, e.g. reflexes exhibited by people sound asleep. Such occurrences present no temptations to confuse them with actions.

20. What is the point of this perhaps tedious classification of what people can do? I gave these examples to lead up to a defence of "epiphenomenalism", promised long ago. Subjective experiences, sensations, feelings, emotions, desires, and the awareness of thought, are by no means "nomological danglers" without function or role.[25] True, they do not enter on their own the causal chains connecting the events of the world, but they do provide agents with reasons for acting, and thus determining, to some extent at least, which causal sequences are to be actualized. My headache, which *is* an epiphenomenon, provides me with a reason for taking aspirin, playing a role thereby in my determination that a Vendler-ingests-absorbs-aspirin-between-t^1-and-t^2

[25] So called by Feigl (in 'The "Mental" and the "Physical"') and Smart (in *Philosophy and Scientific Realism*).

chain (with its appropriate antecedents and consequences) should belong to the causal texture of the cosmos.

We just noted, however, that, at least with respect to certain reflexes, the awareness of the stimulus has no such role to play, since the response is automatic, with no free choice involved. It seems, therefore, that, in these cases at least, the experience is something purely gratuitous, a veritable "dangler" with no use. I do not think this is so, since, although the experience has no influence over that particular response, it retains its function in contributing to the overall state of the agent's consciousness, on the basis of which he can shape his conduct beyond the automatic response. Touching the stove triggers the reflex of pulling back one's hand, and it is painful to boot. If I am right, then the phenomenal pain is not the cause of the reflex, but its memory provides a reason for being more careful in future dealings with the stove.

It appears, then, that the only "function" of the totality of subjective awareness is tied to free action, the spontaneity of the transcendental self manifesting itself in the agency of this or that conscious subject.

21. Long ago we started this whole investigation by considering a cat, an animal, in distress. And, against Descartes and his clan, we defended the cat's right to suffer and to enjoy, e.g. to have genuine pain. Pains and the like, however, turned out to be epiphenomena, standing aloof from the causal processes of nature. Finally, just now, we have found the *raison d'être* for these epiphenomena in the domain of free action. Are cats, then, free agents, or are their pains and pleasures indeed mere "nomological danglers"?

I am by no means an expert on animal (or for that matter human) psychology. Nevertheless, particularly in view of our recent reflections on *actus hominis* versus *actus humani*, I am at least able to suggest some possibilities. What I say of cats (a paradigmatic animal) may be applied to other beasts *mutatis mutandis*, down to Nagel's bat or Austin's cockroach.

First possibility: Descartes was right, cats are mere machines. Of course they are, for physics, biology, etc. (although the stereotype of a machine has to be stretched, but it does not matter). So are humans, however; thus the issue cannot be decided on that level. But we remember from Chapter I, that, in order to find ourselves in the world, we have to endow all "deserving" organisms with inner life. In view of the continuity between human and feline structure and behaviour, there is very little reason to think that cats do not represent "deserving" organisms. *Ergo*: cats have experiences, and the first possibility is better ruled out.

Second possibility: the cat's entire conduct is reflex behaviour accompanied by sensations, feelings, etc. If so, then its inner life is something like a dream: the animal feels things happening to it without any possibility of doing something about them. The cat "feels", (sees, hears, etc.) chasing mice, licking milk, the way we feel our mouths water, hands tremble, or arms stretch out to break a fall.[26]

This is a conceivable situation, and I cannot rule it out. I am disturbed, however, by the utter "uselessness" of experience in this situation. The "epiphenomena" of sensation, feeling, etc., are there completely gratuitously: a subjective "echo" of the physical processes, something to enjoy or to endure in total passivity.

Third possibility: cats are more "human" than our specific pride commonly allows us to admit. Their actions may approximate to our routine activities we mentioned above. In driving a car one does not act in "trance", yet no conscious thoughts concerning the task need cross the driver's mind. His thoughts may be preoccupied with the state of the economy, or engaged in a conversation conducted on the side. Yet not all his reactions are reflexes in the technical sense: he makes decisions to stop or to go through the yellow light, to pass a car now or wait for a safer moment. In a sense he knows what he is doing, and could account for it if asked to. This possibility is tied, of course, to his ability to speak or to communicate by similar means.

Now my suggestion amounts to this: a cat stalking the mouse, climbing the tree, or going through similar routines of his feline existence, "acts" in a similar way. Not in a trance, not by mere reflex; but not with conscious deliberation and preconceived intentions, either. Of course, *he* could not account for his deeds, or even conceive of such an account, since he cannot talk, and, presumably, has no concepts either. Yet—*we* can say—he could have done otherwise, in the same way as the "routine" driver could have stopped at the yellow light. If so, then the "epiphenomena" of the cat's experience do have a role to play, and his conduct is not purely mechanical. The animal is no mere link in the inexorable causal chain of the physical world, but it

---

[26] This seems to be Leibniz's opinion: 'Substantial forms effect no change in the phenomena, any more than do the souls of beasts, if they have souls' (*Discourse*, xii. p. 18).

has a modest influence determining the existence of certain causal sequences.

But then, if we are right about the "access" to our actions, the awareness of some animals cannot be entirely passive and sensory. They must "know" what they are doing in a primitive, preconceptual sense. But, I assume, so do infants. It stands to reason that evolution should pass smoothly through the sharp distinctions we like to draw, both on the ontogenetic and the phylogenetic level.

Bibliography

Adam, Charles, and Tannery, Paul, eds. *Œuvres de Descartes*. Cerf, Paris, 1897–1913.

Anscombe, G. E. M. 'The First Person'. In *Collected Philosophical Papers*, Vol. II. University of Minnesota Press, Minneapolis, 1981.

Aquinas, St. Thomas. *Summa Theologica*. (Fathers of the English Dominican Province, eds.) Benzinger Brothers, New York, etc., 1947–8.

Aristotle. *The Nicomachean Ethics*. (H. Rackham, ed.) Harvard University Press, Cambridge, Mass., 1947.

Austin, J. L. 'A Plea for Excuses'. In *Philosophical Papers*. Clarendon Press, 1961.

Berkeley, George. *Three Dialogues*. See Luce and Jessop, eds. Vol. II.

Brinkley, Robert; Bronaugh, Richard; Marras, Anzonio; eds. *Agent, Action and Reason*. University of Toronto Press, Toronto and Buffalo, 1971.

Black, Max, ed. *Philosophy in America*. Cornell University Press, Ithaca, 1965.

Castañeda, Hector-Neri. ' "He": A Study in the Logic of Self-consciousness'. *Ratio*, viii, 1966, 130–57.

— 'The Logic of Self-Knowledge'. *Nous* I, 9–22.

Chisholm, Roderick. 'Freedom and Action'. In Lehrer, ed.

— *The First Person*. University of Minnesota Press, Minneapolis, 1981.

Cole, Peter, ed. *Syntax and Semantics*, vol. 9: *Pragmatics*. Academic Press, New York, 1978.

Cress, Donald A., ed. *René Descartes, Meditations on First Philosophy*. Hackett, Indianapolis, Cambridge, 1979.

Davidson, Donald. 'Agency'. In Brinkley, *et al.*, eds.

—, and Harman, Gilbert, eds. *Semantics of Natural Language*. D. Reidel Publishing Co., Dordrecht–Boston, 1972.

Dennett, Daniel C. *Brainstorms*. Bradford Books, Montgomery, Vt., 1978.

Descartes, René. See: Adam-Tannery, eds.; Haldane-Ross, eds; Cress, ed.

Donnellan, Keith S. 'Reference and Definite Descriptions'. *Philosophical Review*, lxxv, 1966, 281–304.

— 'Speaking of Nothing'. *Philosophical Review*, lxxxiii, 1974, 3–31.

Feigl, H. 'The "Mental" and the "Physical" '. *Minnesota Studies in the Philosophy of Science*, Vol. II. University of Minnesota Press, Minneapolis, 1958.

Feinberg, Joel. 'Action and Responsibility'. In Black, ed.

Fodor, Jerry A. *The Language of Thought*. Crowell, New York, 1975.

Frankfurt, Harry G. *Demons, Dreamers, and Madmen: The Defense of Reason in Descartes Meditations*, Bobbs-Merrill, Indianapolis, 1970.

Frege, Gottlob. 'The Thought: a Logical Inquiry'. In Strawson, ed.

Grice, H. P. 'Meaning'. *Philosophical Review*, lxvi, 1957, 377–88.

Gunderson, Keith. *Mentality and Machines*. Doubleday & Co., Garden City, NY, 1971.

— ed. *Language, Mind and Knowledge: Minnesota Studies in the Philosophy of Science*, Vol. VII. University of Minnesota Press, Minneapolis, 1975.

Haldane, Elizabeth S., and Ross, G. R. T., eds. *The Philosophical Works of Descartes*. Cambridge University Press, 1931.

Hantikka, Jaakko. '*Cogito Ergo Sum*: Inference or Performance?' *Philosophical Review*, lxxi, 1962, 3–32.

Kant, Immanuel. *Critique of Pure Reason*. See Kemp Smith, ed.

— *Critique of Practical Reason*. (Lewis White Beck, ed.) Bobbs-Merrill, Indianapolis, NY, 1956.

Kaplan, David. 'Dthat'. In Cole, ed.

— 'Quantifying In'. *Synthese 19*, 1968, 178–214.

Kemp Smith, Norman, ed. *Immanuel Kant's Critique of Pure Reason*. Macmillan & Co., London, 1953.

Kripke, Saul. *Naming and Necessity*. Harvard University Press, Cambridge, Mass., 1980.

Lehrer, Keith, ed. *Freedom and Determinism*. Random House, New York, 1966.

Leibniz, G. W. *Discourse on Metaphysics*. In Montgomery, ed.

Lewis, David. *Counterfactuals*. Harvard University Press, Cambridge, Mass., 1973.

— 'Attitudes De Dicto and De Se'. *Philosophical Review*, lxxviii, 1979, 513–43.

Luce, A. A. and Jessop, T. E., eds. *The Works of George Berkeley*. Nelson, London, 1949.

Montgomery, George R. ed. *Leibniz*. Open Court, La Salle, Ill., 1973.

Nagel, Thomas *The Possibility of Altruism*. Princeton University Press, Princeton, NJ, 1970.

— 'What Is It Like to Be a Bat?' *Philosophical Review*, lxiii, 1974, 435–50.

Perry, John 'Frege on Demonstratives'. *Philosophical Review*, lxxxci, 1977, 474–97.

— 'The Problem of the Essential Indexical'. *Nous*, xiii, 1979, 3–21.

Putnam, Hilary. 'The Meaning of "Meaning" '. In Gunderson, ed.

Ross, John Robert. 'Act'. In Davidson and Harman, eds.

Ryle, Gilbert, ed. *Contemporary Aspects of Philosophy*. Oriel Press, Stocksfield, 1977.

Smart, J. J. C. *Philosophy and Scientific Realism*. Routledge and Kegan Paul, New York, 1963.

Strawson, P. F. *Individuals*. Doubleday & Co., Garden City, NY, 1959.

— ed. *Philosophical Logic*. Oxford University Press, 1967.

Vendler, Zeno. *Linguistics in Philosophy*. Cornell University Press, Ithaca and New York, 1968.

— *Res Cogitans*. Cornell University Press, Ithaca and New York, 1972.

— 'On the Possibility of Possible Worlds'. *Canadian Journal of Philosophy*, V, 1975, 57–72.

— 'A Note to the Paralogisms.' In Ryle, ed.

Wittgenstein, Ludwig. *Philosophical Investigations*. (G. E. M. Anscombe, ed.) Blackwell, Oxford, 1953.

— *Tractatus Logico-Philosophicus*. (D. F. Pears and B. F. McGinness, eds.). Routledge and Kegan Paul, New York, 1961.

Index of Names